English in English

The Keys to Unlocking Grammar on the SAT and ACT

By Laura Wilson with Amie Whigham

English in English
The Keys to Unlocking Grammar

By Laura Wilson with Amie Whigham

Published by WilsonDailyPrep
26 S. Greeley Avenue
Chappaqua, NY 10514
www.wilsondailyprep.com
laura@wilsondailyprep.com

© 2008 WilsonDailyPrep, Inc.

Book and cover design by Laura Cacciato
lcacciato@earthlink.net

ISBN: 978-0-615-24317-7

Introduction

Pronouns and adverbs and tense, oh my!

When we think of grammar, we get scared. Why? Because grammar in high school is scary – and **boring.** So – let's be honest – who needs to know grammar when you can just look on the computer for the green squiggles as you are typing an essay? Let the computer fix the mistakes!

However, test takers need to know the rules of English grammar if they want to succeed on test day. So, quick quiz: **Do you know what a contraction is? Pronoun? Preposition?** If your answers are no, no, and definitely not, you're in the same boat as many high school students. Most likely you learned some basic grammar in fourth grade and then quickly moved on to reading *To Kill a Mockingbird* and *Hamlet*, happily replacing grammar rules with plot summaries and themes.

The good news is that you don't need doctorate-level, hard-core grammar to do well on these tests! The key is to understand the questioning patterns – knowing what to look for and how to answer specific repeating types of questions.

This book is meant not only to introduce you to the patterns of both the SAT and ACT, but also to explain some basic (but essential) rules of grammar in a not-a-horrible-lesson-in-English-class type way, so that **you** *(pronoun)* **will** *(tense)* **do** *(verb)* **well** *(adverb)* **on** *(preposition)* **test** *(adjective)* **day** *(noun)*!

Table of Contents

About the Tests

The SAT and ACT are two widely differing college admissions exams. The grammar sections of both are detailed below.

The SAT and ACT are standardized college admissions exams. Although both exams are used to determine college admissions eligibility, the SAT and ACT are fundamentally different: The SAT is a reasoning test, while the ACT is an aptitude test (and more literal). Also, the ACT is a very time-sensitive exam. Some students are naturally "better" at one test and, therefore, **we recommend that all students try both exams.**

KEY STRATEGY

Try both tests.

All students are different: different learning styles, different anxiety-levels, etc. A lot of things factor into why one test is better than the other for a particular student. That is why, once again, it is extremely important to try both tests.

The SAT has three sections: critical reading, math and writing, with a perfect score of 2400. The ACT has four sections: English, math, reading and science, with a perfect score of 36. Although the tests differ, the grammar tested in the writing section of the SAT and the English section of the ACT overlap significantly. The writing and English sections are detailed below.

SAT Writing Component

- Scored out of 800

- 25-minute essay

- 39 multiple-choice questions
    Identifying Sentence Errors – 18 questions
    Improving Sentences – 25 questions
    Improving Paragraphs – 6 questions

The SAT writing component has an essay and two multiple-choice grammar sections. The essay accounts for one-third of the writing score, and the multiple-choice sections for the remaining two-thirds. A perfect score on the writing component is 800.

The score is based on the number of questions answered correctly. Unanswered questions do not negatively affect your score, while incorrect answers result in a 1/4–point deduction. However, **we do not recommend leaving blanks!** "No error" is an answer choice on the SAT: If you do not see an error in the sentence, choose "No error".

The types of grammar questions asked repeat from year to year, and there are many tricks and strategies for *beating this test*. These tricks and strategies are found in this book.

ACT English Section

- Scored out of 36

- 45 minutes

- 75 multiple-choice questions

The ACT English section is strictly multiple choice. Because incorrect answers do not result in any additional point loss, you should answer every question. The questions focus on all aspects of English grammar, with an emphasis on punctuation, and questions can be grouped into rhetoric and mechanics. Rhetoric questions focus on general writing skills and require students to fix transitional sentences, answer main idea questions, and logically reorder paragraphs. Mechanics questions assess a student's understanding of general English grammar. A perfect score on the ACT English section is 36.

KEY STRATEGY

Register for the ACT with writing.

• Please note: The ACT also includes a 30-minute persuasive essay. However, this essay is optional. We recommend all students opt to take the ACT with writing, though, as some colleges require the essay.

A NO-NONSENSE
Grammar Reference Page

- **Nouns:** People, places, or things. *See page 14*

- **Pronouns:** Substitutions for nouns (I, he, she, they, it…). *See page 14*

- **Adjectives:** Descriptions of nouns or pronouns.

- **Verbs:** Action words. *See page 10*

- **Adverbs:** Descriptions of verbs or adjectives, usually ending in –ly. *See page 12*

- **Conjunctions:** Junction or linking words (and, or, but, nor…). *See page 20*

- **Phrases and Clauses:** Wanna-be sentences that just aren't quite there. These are linked on to real-deal sentences by conjunctions, punctuation, or pronouns. Clauses contain a verb. *See page 24*

- **Prepositions:** Little words that give position. These are extremely important to know for both the ACT and SAT. Understanding prepositions and prepositional phrases is the key to unlocking English grammar. *See page 8* for details and exercises. **Memorize the list of prepositions below.**

About	Above	Amid	Around
Against	Along	Before	Behind
As	At	Beside	Between
Below	Beneath	By	Despite
Beyond	During	Except	**For***
Down	In	Inside	Into
From	Near	**Of***	Off
Like	Onto	Opposite	Out
On	Over	Past	Since
Outside	**To***	Toward	Under
Through	Upon	With	Within
Until	Across	After	Underneath

Important to know for tests

The Art of Grammar

The key to success on the grammar sections of both the SAT and ACT is to look and listen.

The writing section of the SAT and the English section of the ACT can be a nightmare for many students because many students do not understand the rules of grammar. But fortunately, the questions asked are not about understanding English grammar. Rather, they are about understanding the patterns of the tests!

KEY STRATEGY

If it sounds wrong, it most likely is wrong.

The grammar sections do not, for the most part, require you to fix the sentence error, only recognize it. Therefore, **if something sounds wrong, it most likely is wrong.** You've been in school for years, hearing proper English, so you know how it should sound. By practicing the grammar sections in both the ACT and the SAT aloud, you'll be able to easily find 60% of the mistakes.

And yes, we know you can't actually read aloud on test day. But you can mumble under your breath! Who cares if the pencil-tapper to your right, the heavy-breather to your left, or the foot-twitcher in front of you thinks you're crazy… You'll be finding the grammar mistakes! And, the more practice, the less mumbling. Your goal is to train your mind and your ear so that you have an **internal grammar voice:** you know what to look for and how it should sound.

Remember, if it sounds wrong, it most likely is wrong.
USE YOUR EARS!

The rest of the book is devoted to the "rules" of English grammar: tips and tricks that you need to beat these tests and catch the remaining 40% of the grammar mistakes! The test questions repeat – OVER and OVER and OVER.

This book will tell you exactly what to look for and how to find the answer, without all the grammar lingo!

Throughout the book, references will be made to the Grammar Keys. It may be helpful to remove the Grammar Key Sheets found on pages 37–41 and keep them handy for reinforcement.

The Sentence Code

The SAT and ACT are written in code – complicated sentence code. You need to understand the nature of the sentence in order to crack this code!

There are four types of sentences: simple, compound, complex and compound-complex.

- A **simple sentence** has a subject and verb: *I ran.*

- A **compound sentence** is constructed by sticking two simple sentences together with a conjunction (and, but, or, nor, for, so, yet): *I ran and I fell.*

- A **complex sentence** has a phrase or clauses attached to the simple sentence: *Because I was late for class, I ran.*

- A **compound-complex sentence** has a phrase or clause attached to a compound sentence: *Because I was late for class, I ran and I fell.*

Obviously, the SAT and ACT use the compound-complex sentences hoping that you'll get lost in the reading and be unable to identify any errors. If the tests were written in simple sentences – well, they would be simple.

KEY STRATEGY

The SAT loves starting sentences with "Because". "Because" at the beginning of a sentence is usually correct!

KEY STRATEGY

Always reduce a complex sentence to its simplest, most basic form.

So here's the trick: **You can reduce any complex sentence to a simple sentence!** This is how you crack the SAT/ACT code. All you have to do is strip off the capes and cloaks of lengthy, flowery writing, and you're left with simple-sentence bases. The next section explains exactly how to strip your sentences down to the bare essentials.

Stripping Your Sentences

It's fairly easy to hear a subject-verb error in a sentence. Test makers know this… and test makers are slightly evil. Therefore, they hide simple subject-verb errors in flowery, complex sentences in which the subject gets lost. It's your job to strip the sentence down to the bare essentials and find the subject!

If Little Miss Sentence wants to walk down the street, she needs to be wearing the basics: pants and a shirt. However, if Little Miss Sentence wants to be trendy, she can accessorize: scarves, necklaces, feather boas, bracelets, hats – the works! But accessories can be overwhelming! **Little Miss Sentence needs to strip down to the basics: a subject and a verb.** Any extras – adjectives, adverbs, prepositional phrases, etc. – need to go! The sentence "striptease" process is detailed below.

▪ Stripping to the Bare Essentials Step 1
Cross out **Prepositional Phrases**
e.g. The bird ~~in the yard~~ began chirping.

This step requires that you know your prepositions! A complete list is found on the No-Nonsense Grammar Reference Page at the beginning of this book, but for the most part, prepositions are little words that give position. "In", "on", "above", "toward", "by" – these guys. The three most commonly used prepositions are **"of", "for"** and **"to"**.

So, a prepositional *phrase* is a preposition with a noun that follows. Prepositional phrases will *never* include the subject of a sentence. Prepositional phrases are strictly accessories used to decorate the subject-containing sentence.

▪ Stripping to the Bare Essentials Step 2
Cross out **Interrupting Phrases**
e.g. The team, ~~ignoring tradition,~~ will update the uniforms.

Interrupting phrases are typically thrown into a sentence between two commas or two dashes. A general rule: **Cross out anything sandwiched between commas.**

However, sometimes longer, flowery sentences have multiple commas that create a sandwich *illusion*. Remember that interrupting phrases are nonessential. If you cross out a portion of the sentence that you believe is sandwiched between two commas, make sure you still have a complete sentence remaining!

e.g. Mowing the lawn, ~~Charles scared his cat~~, venturing out of the garden.

Oops! *Mowing the lawn venturing out of the garden* is NOT a complete sentence. Therefore, *Charles scared his cat* cannot be crossed out! This sentence contains two phrases: *Mowing the lawn* and *venturing out of the garden*. Phrases are nonessential fragments attached to a sentence with commas. The two phrases here, each attached with a comma, create the illusion of a comma sandwich. **You should be left with a complete sentence after crossing out comma sandwiches.** Beginning with a gerund (–ing verb) often indicates a modifying phrase rather than an interrupting phrase. Modification is further discussed on page 24.

Stripping to the Bare Essentials Step 3
Cross out **Nonessentials**

e.g. ~~Early this morning,~~ Emma awoke to finish studying for her difficult chemistry exam.

Other nonessentials include introductory phases (such as "Once upon a time") and most adjectives and adverbs. Nonessential phrases may also be attached to the end of a sentence – so strip from both ends!

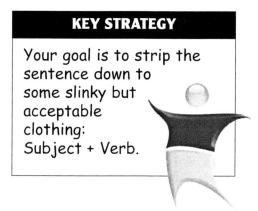

KEY STRATEGY

Your goal is to strip the sentence down to some slinky but acceptable clothing: Subject + Verb.

Verbs

Verbs are action words. The SAT and ACT test several aspects of verbs, including tense, description, and form.

■ Subject-Verb Agreement

Subject-verb agreement is the number-one error on the tests. Always check that subjects and verbs agree!

The SAT loves to put singular subjects with plural verbs and vice versa. You need to always be on the lookout for subject-verb agreement.

1. **Find the subject of the sentence.** *(Refer to Stripping Sentences on page 8)*
    a. Strip out prepositional phrases
    b. Strip out interrupting phrases
    c. Strip out beginning or concluding phrases

2 **Determine whether the subject is singular or plural.** Remember that collective nouns, nouns referring to a group as a whole, are singular! *(See page 16.)*

3. **Make sure that singular subjects are paired with singular verbs, and that plural subjects are paired with plural verbs.**
    "Either", "Neither" and "Each" are tricky: they all take the singular form of the verb *(See page 17).*

Sentence: *The books on the shelf in the library needs dusting.*
Stripped: The books needs dusting.
Corrected: **The books need dusting.**

Sentence: *Scott and Allison, hoping to win the lottery, buys tickets each week.*
Stripped: Scott and Allison buys tickets each week.
Corrected: **Scott and Allison buy tickets each week.**

Notice how awful English grammar truly is. Subject-verb agreement gets tricky because to pluralize a noun you add an "s". To pluralize a verb, you *take off* the "s". To keep things straight in your head, think "he" for singular nouns and "they" for plural. This makes it easier to decide if your verb agrees.

KEY STRATEGY

Always check subject-verb agreement first.

KEY STRATEGY

Think "He" for singular nouns and "They" for plural so that you can easily hear subject-verb errors.

Of course, the tests don't want to make it easy for you to catch subject-verb errors. Therefore, they add in a little twist: *inverted word order*. **Inverted word order refers to a sentence that places the verb *before* the subject.**

<table>
<tr><td>

KEY STRATEGY

Pay attention to inverted
word order:
There is vs. There are
There has vs. There have
There was vs. There were

</td></tr>
</table>

For example: *There were two books on the shelf.* "Were" – the verb – is placed before "two books" – the subject.

Also, notice that the sentence begins "There were". "There" often indicates inverted word order, so pay attention to "there is", "there are", "there was", "there were", "there has", and "there have". Inverted word order simply makes it a little trickier to catch the mistake, so watch out!

Active and Passive Voice

Verbs are action words — use the active voice.

On both the SAT and ACT, you always want your verbs to be active, because active verbs are powerful. **You want to punch a reader in the face, not wink at him.** Both active and passive voices are grammatically correct, but the **tests like active voice.** Take a look at the following:

Passive... wink wink
Jim was hit by Jack.
The ball was hit by Tommy.
The door was slammed by Carol.

Active... wham!
Jack hit Jim.
Tommy hit the ball.
Carol slammed the door.

Passive voice does not impact a reader. Active voice, however, does and is therefore more powerful. Always use the active voice! Notice that the passive voice is longer and usually contains "by". On both the SAT and ACT, the shorter answer is usually right. **Shortest is sweetest!**

<table>
<tr><td>

KEY STRATEGY

Shortest is
sweetest!

</td></tr>
</table>

Verb Tenses

Verb tenses are a piece of cake if you have a fine-tuned grammar ear. If not, keep in mind the simple tricks below, and you'll be all set for test day.

There are several verb tenses. The simplest are past, present, and future: *I did, I do,* and *I will do,* respectively. The more troublesome tenses are the "perfect" tenses: tenses that combine the past with present, past with past, or present with future.

<table>
<tr><td>

KEY STRATEGY

Keep tense
consistent.

</td></tr>
</table>

Past Perfect – *I had done*

Present Perfect – *I have done*

Future Perfect – *I will have done*

The SAT tries to trip you up by throwing in a bunch of actions together and letting you fumble around with the tenses. A rule of thumb: Keep the tense the same throughout the sentence/paragraph/essay.

A trick to finding some of the SAT's tense errors is to watch out for "would" and "will". Often "would" and "will" are incorrectly switched.

<table>
<tr><td>

KEY STRATEGY

"Would" vs. "Will"
Always look twice at
these when underlined
in a sentence.

</td><td>

For example:

The boy thinks that <u>it would have rained</u> tomorrow.

-OR-

The boy thinks that <u>it will rain</u> tomorrow.

</td></tr>
</table>

The second sentence is correct. Tomorrow indicates the future, so you want "will rain", the future tense. Tense errors are often difficult to catch because you really have to hear the mistake. Before you pick "No error" on the SAT, go back and double check that all tenses are correct. Often the questions will give you a clue to tense — a date! Therefore, **circle dates or time periods mentioned; these are clues to tense!**

KEY STRATEGY

Circle all numbers and dates.

To Win or At Winning?

Become a pro at spotting underlined verbs in the "to - " form (infinitive verb) and the "-ing" form (gerund verb). You don't need to understand gerund and infinitive grammar mumbo-jumbo, but you do need to be thinking "to vs. ing". Whenever you see a *"to" verb* or an *"ing" verb* underlined, ask yourself if it should be switched.

For example:

The computer is <u>good to calculate</u> problems.

-OR-

The computer is <u>good at calculating</u> problems.

KEY STRATEGY

"TO" vs. "ING"
Always switch "to"
verbs to "ing" verbs
and vice versa
to see which
sounds better.

Hopefully you can hear that the second sentence sounds better, and is therefore correct. Also, notice that the preposition "at" was slipped in when "to calculate" was changed to "calculating". Often when changing from "to" to "ing" you'll need to put a preposition in: *The computer is good calculating problems* will never sound correct! **So remember your prepositions!**

Describing Verbs

Words used to describe verbs are called *adverbs*. As a general rule, adverbs are words that end in –ly. For example, *I ran quickly*. If you see an adverb (word ending in –ly) underlined, it's probably not wrong. **The SAT will leave off the –ly ending on one or two words per test.** If there are words describing any sort of action, they need to end in –ly!

KEY STRATEGY

Love-ly words!
When in doubt, go
with the –ly ending.

Irregular Verbs

Sometimes a form of a verb just isn't what you'd expect. Of course, these are the verbs that are constantly used on both the SAT and ACT.

Below is a list of common irregular verbs – verbs that just never sound right. Irregular verbs should definitely be reviewed. Memorize the list below, because although "swum", "drunk", and "rung" may sound funny, they are correct in certain tenses.

PRESENT	PAST	PAST PARTICIPLE
Arise	Arose	Arisen
Bring	Brought	Brought
Choose	Chose	Chosen
Dive	Dove or Dived	Dived
Draw	Drew	Drawn
Drink	Drank	Drunk
Drive	Drove	Driven
Eat	Ate	Eaten
Fall	Fell	Fallen
Fly	Flew	Flown
Freeze	Froze	Frozen
Give	Gave	Given
Get	Got	Gotten
Go	Went	Gone
Grow	Grew	Grown
Hang (thing)	Hung	Hung
Hang (person)	Hanged	Hanged
Know	Knew	Known
Lay	Laid	Laid
Lie	Lay	Lain
Ride	Rode	Ridden
Ring	Rang	Rung
Rise	Rose	Risen
Run	Ran	Run
See	Saw	Seen
Shrink	Shrank	Shrunk
Slay	Slew	Slain
Speak	Spoke	Spoken
Spring	Sprang	Sprung
Steal	Stole	Stolen
Swim	Swam	Swum
Take	Took	Taken
Tear	Tore	Torn
Weave	Wove	Woven
Write	Wrote	Written

Pronouns

Most likely "pronoun" was a 4th grade vocabulary word that you never needed to worry about afterwards...until now.   He, she, it, you, us, they, them, etc. – these are pronouns.

■ Promiscuous Pronouns

Promiscuous: characterized by or involving indiscriminate mingling or association

Pronouns are words that take the place of specific nouns. (Remember that a noun is a person, place or thing.) So, instead of saying: *Bobby ate cake. Bobby got sick and Bobby couldn't go to school*, you could say: *Bobby ate cake. He got sick and he couldn't go to school*. In the sentence above, the pronoun "he" takes the place of the noun "Bobby".

A pronoun must take the place of one, and only one, specific noun!

If a pronoun is going with all sorts of nouns, it is a promiscuous pronoun, and this is a very bad thing. If you can't tell what the pronoun is taking the place of – another bad thing. And finally, if the pronoun does not agree with the noun – yet another bad thing.

Watch out for the above errors. They are very simple but very easy to overlook.
Always check pronouns twice in the grammar section and make sure they are correct! (Make sure to especially double check "it". "It" is the most promiscuous pronoun on both tests!)

■ Pronoun Cases

Depending on the noun it is substituting in for, a pronoun will be one of three cases:
Nominative: The subject
Objective: The thing being acted upon
Possessive: Showing ownership

Nominative	I	We	You	He/She/It	They	Who
Objective	Me	Us	You	Him/Her/It	Them	Whom
Possessive	My	Our	Your	His/Her/Its	Their	Whose

Memorize the above chart. There are three general rules to figure out the correct pronoun case, as detailed on the next page.

Case Rule 1

When more than one person is mentioned, cross off the other person and see if the sentence makes sense. Use your ear!

He asked the accountant and ME / I to go.
He asked ~~the accountant and~~ ME / I to go.
He asked the accountant and me to go.

Peter and ME / I are going to the movies.
~~Peter and~~ ME / I are (am) going to the movies.
Peter and I are going to the movies.

When did you last write a letter to Anne and HE / HIM?
When did you last write a letter to ~~Anne and~~ HE / HIM?
When did you last write a letter to Anne and him?

Case Rule 2

There are two ways to understand Rule 2. You can either memorize that any comparison ending in a pronoun takes the nominative form – or better, method 2. **When a comparison is implied and ends with a pronoun, finish off the comparison and you will hear the error. Use your ear!**

> **KEY STRATEGY**
>
> Zero in on comparative words in a sentence and make sure comparisons are "finished off".

Joan had more experience than SHE / HER.
Joan had more experience than SHE / HER had experience.
Joan had more experience than she.

Lindsey can eat as much as ME / MYSELF / I.
Lindsey can eat as much as ME / MYSELF / I can eat.
Lindsey can eat as much as I.

Case Rule 3

Prepositions **always** take the objective case. Prepositions, again, are those little words that typically indicate position. "Of", "for" and "to" are the most popular prepositions on the tests. You can't use your ear on this one, so **you must memorize this rule!**

> **KEY STRATEGY**
>
> It is easy to hear the mistake for most prepositional comparisons. "To me"... "For me"..."From him", etc. The tricky one is "between". "Between" always takes the objective case. It's always between you and me, <u>NOT</u> between you and I.

The card is for HIM / HE.
Objective case: HIM
The card is for him.

The bug was on ME / I.
Objective case: ME
The bug was on me.

Larry is between you and ME / I.
Objective case: ME
Larry is between you and me.

■ Collective Nouns

Be especially careful when using the pronouns "they" and "it". Collective nouns are meant to trick you!

The SAT loves using collective nouns. These are nouns that are singular, but collectively include multiple items. For example, *the team was supposed to compete Friday but it had to forfeit.*

KEY STRATEGY

It vs. They
"It" is a singular pronoun, whereas "they" is plural.

Watch out for collective nouns! You'll want to refer to these nouns as "they", but **collective nouns are singular** and take the pronoun "it".

Always double check pronouns - triple check "it" and "they".

Common Collective Nouns:

Team, Committee, Company, Board,
Group, Species, Crowd, Troupe, Band,
City, Town, State, Country, Family

■ Who vs. Whom

Test-makers know that most test-takers have no clue when to use the pronoun "whom". Don't fall into thetet-takers' traps!

If you can take out the "who"/"whom" in the question and substitute "he"/"they", then "WHO" is appropriate. If you can substitute "him"/"them", then "WHOM" is appropriate.

Sentence in Question: *Joe and Mark,* WHO/WHOM *are athletes, competed in the race.*
Substitution: Joe and Mark, THEY are athletes, competed in the race.
Correct Sentence: Joe and Mark, **who are athletes**, competed in the race.

Sentence in Question: *Cindy is going with* WHO/WHOM *to the prom?*
Substitution: Cindy is going with (him) to the prom?
Correct Sentence: Cindy is going **with whom** to the prom?

■ Special Pronouns: Either, Neither, Each

"Either", "neither" and "each" are tricky little pronouns. They ALWAYS take the singular verb. Once again, **"either", "neither", and "each" take the singular verb!** This is a nit-picky grammar rule that sounds wrong, so you can't use your ear. Memorize that "either", "neither" and "each" are singular.*

*There are exceptions, but these exceptions are not on the SAT or ACT.

> **KEY STRATEGY**
>
> "Either", "Neither" and "Each" are Singular.

To figure out singular vs. plural verb forms, find the verb and think "he" vs. "they". "He" always takes the singular verb, and "they" always takes the plural verb. So, for "either", "neither" and "each" you want the "he" (singular) form of the verb. This should make it a little easier on your brain!

Sentence:	*Either the tape or the CD make a terrific gift.*
Think:	He makes/They make
Corrected:	**Either the tape or the CD makes a terrific gift.**

Sentence:	*Neither the tennis ball nor the net are in good condition.*
Think:	He is/They are
Corrected:	**Neither the tennis ball nor the net is in good condition.**

There are a handful of other special pronouns. These are not found on the SAT or ACT as much as "either", "neither", and "each", but they do appear every so often, and are important for general good writing.

■ **Everyone**	singular
■ **Every**	singular
■ **Everybody**	singular
■ **Anyone**	singular
■ **No one**	singular
■ **Nobody**	singular
■ **None**	singular or plural
■ **Any**	singular or plural
■ **Some**	singular or plural
■ **All**	singular or plural

Parallelism

The SAT loves balanced sentences!

■ Equalizing AND

"And" is an equal sign on both the SAT and ACT. **Whatever is found on one side of the "and" must be found on the other.** This rule also holds true for "but", "yet", "so", "for", and "or" – "and" is just more common.

If a preposition is on one side of the "and", make sure you have a preposition on the other side. If there is a gerund or infinitive ("-ing" or "to-" verb) on one side, make sure you have a gerund or infinitive on the other side.

For example:

> The nanny was hired to watch the children, to clean the house, and for cooking meals.
>
> -OR-
>
> The nanny was hired to watch the children, to clean the house, and to cook meals.

The second sentence is correct. Notice the parallel construction around "and": to watch, to clean, AND to cook.

> She liked to watch TV and she liked reading.
>
> -OR-
>
> She liked to watch TV and she liked to read.

Again the second sentence is correct: to watch AND to read. Nice and equal. In keeping things balanced and parallel, be sure to always pair active voice with active voice.

> The ball was hit by Mary and Jim caught the ball.
>
> -OR-
>
> Mary hit the ball and Jim caught the ball.

The first sentence pairs a passive voice clause with an active voice clause. This is incorrect. The second sentence exhibits parallelism by balancing active voice clauses – and this is correct.

■ Hand Holders

When constructing a balanced sentence, some words go hand-in-hand to create parallelism.

Hand holders are correlative conjunctions. All you need to know is that you cannot break the buddy system for the following:

- **Not Only ... But Also**
- **Neither ... Nor**
- **Either ... Or**
- **Both ... And**
- **To ... From**

Whenever you see one of the above in a sentence, you'd best find its partner!

For Example:

The senator was pleased <u>not only</u> with voter turnout, <u>but also</u> with voter support of her proposal.

<u>Neither</u> Frank <u>nor</u> Stella arrived to work on time.

Sara was going to order <u>either</u> the steak <u>or</u> the salmon.

Conjunctions

"Conjunction junction, what's your function?" Conjunctions are connection words. Their function is to put two ideas together, and they are used to construct balanced parallel sentences.

AND

"And" is the most common conjunction you will encounter on these tests. Remember, "and" is an equal sign.

KEY STRATEGY

All conjunctions function as equal signs, combining parallel-structured ideas.

BUT

"But" is also a conjunction. Unlike "and", which attaches two related ideas, "but" is used to put together two contrasting ideas.

OR

"Or" is commonly used in lists on the SAT and ACT. It is also used to relate two alternates. In this case, "or" is often paired with "either".

For example:

> *I wasn't allowed to eat meat, fish,* **or** *poultry on this diet.*

> *I could have gone* **either** *to the movies* **or** *to Mike's party.*

NOR

"Nor" is the negated form of "or". It is used when you're discussing negated statements. "Nor" is often paired with "neither".

KEY STRATEGY

"Either" goes with "Or".
"Neither" goes with "Nor".

For example:

> *I was so depressed that I could* **not** *sleep,* **nor** *could I eat.*

> *The rain was* **neither** *needed* **nor** *pleasant.*

There are also many other conjunctions that may be used to put clauses together. These are typically linked to the sentence with a comma and are addressed under "modification" (*See page 24*). "For", "yet", and "so", other common conjunctions, are not detailed in this section because they are not commonly seen on either test.

Comparisons

Never compare apples to sailboats on these tests. Comparisons should be parallel, just as clauses around conjunctions should be.

■ "Than" and "As"

"Than" and "as" are the two staple comparison words. Get in the habit of circling these as you come across them in the grammar sections of both tests. If you see "than" or "as", a comparison is being made. **All comparisons need to be parallel!**

Make sure your comparisons make sense! You want to compare shoes to shoes, money to money, etc. Sometimes, however, a comparison is not so obvious. **If the comparison is positioned at the end of the sentence and is implied, finish the sentence to make sure your comparison is parallel.** This is a huge key!

For example:
The judges felt that Brian's cake tasted better than Joe.

In this sentence, a cake is incorrectly compared to a person. This is difficult to hear at first, but, if you finish the sentence, the mistake becomes obvious.

The judges felt that <u>Brian's cake</u> tasted better <u>than Joe's cake</u>.

Another example:
Reports show that a sales representative's salary is higher than a doctor.

Sounds OK at first, but again, finish off the sentence to ensure a parallel comparison.

Reports show that a sales representative's <u>salary</u> is higher <u>than</u> a doctor's <u>salary</u>.

Another key with comparisons:
SHORTEST IS SWEETEST DOES NOT APPLY TO COMPARISONS.
Often the longest answer is correct because comparisons need to be completed.

■ Like...totally!

"Like" is almost never correct on the SAT or ACT. When making a comparison on the SAT, you should stick to "as" or "than". The tests check for "valley girl" talk, so like, don't like pick "like", like it'll be like totally wrong. Point made.

On a more serious note, "like" is acceptable if you are comparing two "unlike" things: *My love is like a red, red rose.* It may also be used as a preposition.

Sarah, like Billy, hates seafood..

■ Comparatives and Superlatives

Comparatives are the "mores" and superlatives are the "mosts".

You don't have to know what a comparative and superlative are for these tests. **You do need to know the key: more vs. most.**

KEY STRATEGY
"More" vs. "Most"

Comparatives are words used to express a comparison between two things.

The apple is redder than the strawberry. The girl is taller than the boy.

These are your "more" comparisons. (The apple is more red than the strawberry. The girl is more tall than the boy.) Remember, **the comparative (more) is used when you're dealing with TWO things.**

Superlatives, then, are the "mosts". Superlatives are used to express a comparison among a group of things – more than two!

KEY STRATEGY
Circle Numbers

Of the three girls, Jane is the <u>tallest</u> (most tall).

A little trick – **pay attention to numbers**. Then you'll know if you're dealing with two or more than two, and know to use the comparative or superlative! Numbers also help with subject-verb agreement!

Punctuation

Punctuation errors are much more prevalent on the ACT than on the SAT. You should focus specifically on commas and semicolons for the SAT.

The Confusing Comma

Commas can be your worst nightmare or best friend on these exams. Commas are thrown into sentences at random and you need to be able to pick out which ones should stay and which ones should go. There are several comma rules to understand, so make sure you and the rules are buddy-buddy.

■ The Mother of all Comma Rules

A comma alone cannot separate two complete sentences. The separation of two sentences by a comma only (no "and", "because", "which", etc...just a comma) is incorrect. **This rule has no exceptions.**

Mark loves cheese, Mary hates it.

■ The List Comma Rule

Any list requires commas between the listed items. These items can be nouns, adjectives, verbs, etc.

Milk, bread, eggs and cheese.

The big, brown, fuzzy bear.

This is an easy rule. The commas that separate items of a list are unaffected by the remaining comma rules below. **A list comma is a list comma – that's it.**

■ The Comma Sandwich Rule

Two commas are used to surround, or sandwich, sentence accessories. These accessories should be stripped off the sentence. *(Refer to "sentence stripping" on page 8.)* **You should be able to cross out anything in between two commas and have a nice-sounding sentence left. If you cross something out and you are left without a sentence, then either there should not be a comma there, or it's an illusory sandwich** *(see page 9).*

For example:

> Stella, possibly the best vocalist on campus, was expelled yesterday.
>
> Stripped: Stella was expelled yesterday.

Remember, if you can't get rid of everything that's sandwiched between two commas, then you can't have two commas! For those grammar gurus out there, a subtle catch to this rule – **prepositional phrases do not get sandwiched in between commas.** Remember, a prepositional phrase begins with a preposition and can be stripped out of a sentence. If it is already removable, I don't need to use punctuation that says "remove me" as two commas do.

■ The "Comma And" Rule

This is a tricky but simple rule. The "Comma And", "Comma Or", and "Comma But" rules are all the same. If you have a conjunction (and, or, but) separating two complete sentences then you need to place a comma before the conjunction. Put simply, "comma and" = "period". **If you don't have a complete sentence on both sides of the conjunction, no comma is required.**

For example:

Sentence: *Michelle, and her boyfriend Kyle went rafting.*
Think: Michelle. Her boyfriend Kyle went rafting. – **incorrect**
Corrected: **Michelle and her boyfriend Kyle went rafting.**

Sentence: *The leaves on the trees are starting to turn colors, and the nights are getting longer and longer.*
Think: The leaves on the trees are starting to turn colors. The nights are getting longer and longer. – **correct**
Corrected: **As is.**

Understanding this rule is a huge help for the ACT English section.

■ The Single Comma Rule

You don't want random commas inserted all over the place. One comma is used to indicate where the reader should logically pause. Generally, **the one-comma rule applies to intro phrases and modification.**

There's nothing wrong with modification. However, *dangling* modification is a **huge** error on the SAT grammar section. A dangling modifier is a non-sentence clause "dangling" off of the real sentence by a comma. **You don't want your modifiers dangling!** For modification to be correct, the subject of the non-sentence clause must be found directly after the comma. See "sentence stripping" *(page 8)* for more details.

For example:

Because she was hungry, the pizza looked amazingly good to Sarah.

-OR-

Because she was hungry, Sarah thought the pizza looked amazingly good.

At first, both sentences look correct. Realize that "because she was hungry" is not a sentence! It's dangling off the real sentence by a comma! Whoopie! Modification! Circle the comma, and draw an arrow to what follows. Sarah, or "she", is the subject of the modifier. Therefore, "Sarah" or "she" must be found directly after the comma. **Only the second sentence is correct.**

Sometimes the modifier comes **AFTER** the sentence base, creating reverse modification. This modifier still needs to be stuck onto the sentence with a comma. In this case, the subject of the modifier must be found directly **BEFORE** the comma.

Clauses often begin with subordinating conjunctions. Subordinating conjunctions are so termed because they are weak! They are holding on to the *dominant* sentence with a comma. "Because", "Since", "Whereas" and "After" are common examples of subordinating conjunctions. These may come before or after the sentence base; when they come before, they will be linked with a comma.

For example:

After they had dinner, they went dancing.

They went dancing after they had dinner.

The Simple Semicolon

The semicolon obeys one simple rule. The SAT Writing section loves semicolons! Look at answer choices that have semicolons first...they're usually correct (if they follow the cardinal rule below).

■ The Cardinal Semicolon Rule

KEY STRATEGY

A semicolon **must** have a complete sentence on both sides.

Semicolons are used in place of periods. They separate two complete sentences. There must be a complete sentence on both sides of the semicolon!

For example:

The boy was hungry; he went to the store and bought ice cream.

All mammals have hair on their bodies; all reptiles are cold-blooded.

Please note: There are some additional, more subtle rules that apply to semicolons; however, these rules do not apply to the ACT or SAT.

The Annoying Apostrophe

Apostrophes are much more an ACT problem than an SAT problem. However, it's good to know when apostrophes are appropriate as a general good-writing skill.

■ The Contraction Rule

Contractions involve two words smushed together, with some of the letters pulled out. "I'm", "Couldn't", "Let's", etc. are all contractions. The most important contraction you need to know for the ACT is "it's".

It's = It is.

■ The Possession Rule

KEY STRATEGY

Do not confuse "it's" with "its"
"It's" = it is
"Its" is possessive

Apostrophes can be used to show ownership when coupled with an "s". The apostrophe-s rules can get confusing, so be careful.

Generally, **"'s"** is translated into "owns something". For example, *Mike's bike* – Mike owns the bike. The dog's collar – the dog owns the collar.

There are a few exceptions, with it's/its being most important.

Once again **"it's" = "it is". "Its" = "it owns something".**

When correcting apostrophe problems, first ask yourself if anything owns anything else. If not, then no apostrophe is needed. **If possession is being indicated, then you need an apostrophe.**
If a word ends with an "s", just add an apostrophe to the end of the word, not apostrophe-s (Mr. Roberts owns the book. Mr. Roberts' book.) In general, an apostrophe found after an "s" indicates plurality.* For example: The elephants' habitat.

The Box Method

To figure out where exactly the apostrophe goes, use the "box method". Simply box in the word in question, stopping before the apostrophe. If this boxed-in word makes sense, then the apostrophe is in the correct position. If this boxed word does not make sense, you need to move the apostrophe.

The ⬚familys⬚' boat – the word ends with the apostrophe. So, the familys own the boat. Familys is not a word... it needs to be "families" if multiple families own a boat. Therefore, the apostrophe is in the wrong spot because the word does not make sense.

The ⬚family⬚'s boat – the word ends with the apostrophe. So, the family owns the boat. Makes sense...the apostrophe is in the right spot.

The ⬚boys⬚' clubhouse – Once again, the word in question ends with the apostrophe. So, the boys own the clubhouse. If the apostrophe remains in this spot, then the sentence would be referring multiple boys, and their clubhouse.

The ⬚boy⬚'s clubhouse – Here, again the word ends with the apostrophe. So, the boy owns the clubhouse. An apostrophe in this spot would indicate that the clubhouse belongs to a single boy.

Colons and Dashes – The Oddballs

Colons and dashes are rarely, if ever, used or tested on the SAT. You will see them on the ACT, however. If you can avoid using either one, do so. Dashes and colons are "oddballs" in punctuation, with lots of specific little rules and exceptions. The general usage is described below.

■ The Colon Rules

Colons are used to indicate that a definition, explanation or list is to follow. They may or may not separate two complete sentences. Rather than memorize the subtleties of all the colon rules, pick colons by default on the ACT if nothing else works.

To indicate a definition

Perspicacity: wisdom.

To indicate a list

I had to buy several things at the grocery store: milk, eggs, cheese, and bread.

To indicate an explanation

My mother and I did not get along when I was a teenager: I was angry with her for divorcing my father.

■ The Dash Rules

Dashes, for the most part, work like commas. Anything in between two dashes can be crossed out, and one dash can separate an introductory phrase. If you start extra information with a dash, stick to using the dash. If you start extra information with a comma, stick to using a comma. (Honestly though, if you have no idea what punctuation to use, use the dash!) Dashes are kind of the "catch-all". If nothing else works, the dash will. Again, like the colon, rather than memorizing exactly when and how we use the dash – pick the dash by default. If nothing else works, pick the dash!

Transitions

Coherence and flow are two crucial elements to writing: Ideas should be linked with transitional words and phrases. Transitions are tested heavily on the ACT.

Transitions allow a reader to prepare for a reversal in thought or a continuance in thought. For some reason, coming up with transitions is difficult for many high schoolers. The nice thing about the SAT and ACT is that they give you the transitions – you just have to pick one!

Several common transitional words and phrases are categorized below:

Thought Continuers	Thought Reversers
Furthermore	However
In addition	On the other hand
Moreover	Although
Similarly	Conversely
And/Also	Nevertheless
Likewise	Nonetheless
First/Second/Third/Finally	But/Yet
Consequently	On the contrary

There are many questions about transitions on the ACT. The trick to getting these transitional questions correct is to ignore the complicated writing of the sentence in question, and to use your own simple little sentence. Use the transitions in your sentence.

For example, take a look at the ACT-style question below. Correct the underlined portion of the sentence. If you believe the underlined portion is correct, select "no change".

The stories she held so dear were tales of life and death; they told of time; they told of love; they told of self-realization. **However,** *she was hesitant to share the stories of her people with her own children.*
>   A. No Change
>   B. Furthermore
>   C. Consequently
>   D. Moreover

Ugh! Look at that sentence – way too complicated. Try this sentence instead: **Apples are crisp and delicious.** Using this short and sweet sentence, plug in the transitions, and finish the sentence off. This will allow you to determine the function of each transitional word without getting a headache.

Apples are crisp and delicious; HOWEVER, they can rot out your teeth.

You're reversing the line of thought. You started with good things and ended with bad things. "However" is a thought-reverser.

Apples are crisp and delicious; FURTHERMORE, they were voted fruit of the year!

You're continuing along the same line of thought. Good to good.

Apples are crisp and delicious; CONSEQUENTLY, apples are the world's favorite fruit.

Again, continuing. You start off with good things, and you end with good things.

Apples are crisp and delicious; MOREOVER, they are the perfect snack size.

Continuing.

Jot down a C for thought-continuer, or R for thought-reverser next to the answer choices. Notice the pattern – you've got three continuers and one reverser. More than likely the correct answer is the odd guy out! And examining the original sentence, it goes from stories held dear to stories that aren't to be told – a good thing to a bad thing. "However" is the correct transition needed.

Diction

Diction refers to word usage. On the SAT and ACT, there are two major types of word-usage errors: using the completely wrong word or using too many words.

■ Using The Wrong Word

KEY STRATEGY

Diction errors occur once per exam.

On the SAT, there will be one question per test that uses an incorrect word in a sentence. Often, you're reading so fast that your brain subconsciously fixes the error, **so look out for that one diction question!**

For Example:

> After World War II, every European country accept Switzerland suffered economically.

"Accept", meaning "to take in", should be replaced with "except", meaning "but". Accept/Except is a common diction error on the SAT. Below are two other common diction errors.

"Of" vs. "Have" – Do not use "of" as a verb! "Might of" is **never** correct. "Might have", "Will have" and "Would have" are correct. And of course, "of" will sound correct because of the contraction forms: Might've, would've, could've, etc. Don't be fooled. **The ACT will ask one question per test that deals with "of" vs. "have".**

"Declining" vs. "Reclining" – "Declining" indicates a decrease, while "reclining" is used to describe someone lounging in a chair. Go with "declining" on these tests!

Below is a list of other common diction errors. These are "silly" mistakes on the test, and extremely difficult to catch.

Formally/Formerly	**Quiet/Quite**	**Disinterested/Uninterested**
Implicit/Explicit	**Altar/Alter**	**Beside/Besides**
Infer/Refer	**Adapt/Adopt**	**Elicit/Illicit**
Compose/Comprise	**Assure/Insure/Ensure**	

Using Too Many Words

Redundancy, repeating words in writing, is a huge ACT problem. Redundancy is also easy to miss, so be on the look out. **Remember – shortest is sweetest.** Choose the shortest answer on the ACT to avoid redundancy! (On the SAT, too, but redundancy is more prevalent on the ACT.)

Examples of redundant sentences:

The archer, with his bow and arrows, stood watch at the castle gate.

Hello! An archer is a person with a bow and arrows. Obviously he is with his bow and arrows. The portion of the sentence within the commas is redundant.

The mountain was pine-covered and forested – animals hid easily.

If the mountain is covered in pine trees, it must be forested. And if there is a forest, well, there are probably pine trees. Delete one or the other to avoid redundancy!

The gas supply was sufficient enough for the drive home.

What does "sufficient" mean? "Enough".
What does "enough" mean? "Sufficient".
Redundant!

Double Negatives

Another diction trap is the double negative. **If you don't have nothing – then you have something.** Watch for "scarcely", "hardly", and "no" put together. These words form common double negatives tested on both exams.

For example:

The store had scarcely no milk.

Well then, the store had a lot of milk. This may be confusing at first, but reason it out and you'll see the problem. If there is "scarcely no", or "barely no", then there's only a tiny bit of none, leaving a lot of some. Don't drive yourself crazy working out the logic of this – just remember the key!

The 'W' Page

Some huge keys on these tests are 'w' words. Watch out for them!

All of the following are KEYS to both the SAT and ACT. **Memorize the rules below!**

KEY STRATEGY

Memorize each of the 'W' keys.

▦ WHERE

"Where" is almost always incorrect. **"Where" should only be used to express direction and location!**

▦ WHICH

"Which" is a WITCH! **"Which" must be used in conjunction with a preposition** to be correct on the SAT/ACT. This means that "in which", "of which", "by which", etc. are great… but "which" alone is wrong! Also, "which" is never used for people – "whom" should be used instead.

On a side note, "that" is a much better word than "which". **The SAT loves "that".** "Which" creates nonessential clauses, while "that" creates essential clauses. Of course, there are some exceptions to this rule, and occasionally "which" without a preposition will be correct. But in general – 9 times out of 10 – go with "that" rather than "which"!

KEY STRATEGY

The SAT loves "that". If "that" is underlined, it is usually correct.

▦ WHILE

"While" is a tricky one! Technically, **"while" should only be used to indicate time.** Most often, "while" should be replaced with "although", "but", "and", "or".

▦ WOULD vs. WILL

This key is explained in the verb tense section. **Always double check "would" and "will"** in a sentence; sometimes they're switched!

▦ W…Being

OK, "being" starts with a 'b', but it's just as bad as the "w" words, if not worse. "Being" is a bad, bad thing on these tests. **DO NOT choose answer choices containing "being".**

Idioms

Idioms are the hardest things to catch on the grammar sections. Look for them before you choose "No error"!

Idioms are idiotic grammar rules. They are language quirks – grammatically correct for no grammatical reason. There are simple idioms (figurative rather than literal expressions, such as "You're a pain in the neck") and then there are subtle idioms.

The subtle, more difficult idiomatic expressions involve only two or three words. These are the idioms the tests like to throw at you. **Typically, they contain prepositions.** Before you choose "No error", double check any underlined preposition. Changing one little preposition can convey a completely new meaning: **"throw up", "throw out", "throw toward".** So, it is very important you know your prepositions.

Memorize the list of prepositions found at the beginning of this book! *(page 5)*
Below is a list of common idiomatic expressions.

Idiomatic (correct)	**Unidiomatic** (incorrect)
Die of	Die with
Authority on	Authority about
Equally bad	Equally as bad
In accordance with	In accordance to
In search of	In search for
Independent of	Independent from
Prior to	Prior than
Seldom if ever	Seldom or ever
Superior to	Superior than
Different from	Different than
Consists of	Consists in
Proponent of	Proponent for
Preoccupied with	Preoccupied in
Familiarity with	Familiarity of

The Winning SAT Strategy

▤ FIRST

1. Read the sentence quickly but carefully.
2. **Use your ear!** If something sounds wrong, it most likely is.
3. **Strip it, baby!** Remove the nonessentials from your sentence and locate your subject.
4. **Check subject-verb agreement.**
5. **Double check ALL underlined pronouns.**

▤ THEN

For the Find the Error Section:

▤ Look for the Keys!

▤ Double check underlined prepositions for IDIOMS.

▤ "No error" is correct for about 1 in 5 questions. Don't be afraid to pick it!

For the Fix the Sentence Section:

▤ This section revolves around the comma splice. **Circle any commas in the sentence.** Ask yourself, am I dealing with dangling modification or do I have a comma in between two complete sentences? (Both of these are bad, bad things.)

▤ Skim the answer choices.

▤ **Get rid of any answer choices with "BEING" in them.** "WHICH" without a preposition and "WHERE" are usually wrong as well. Cross off answer choices with either of those.

- **The SAT loves semicolons.** Look first at answers with semicolons – remember, a semicolon separates two complete sentences.

- **Look at the shortest answers first!** Shortest is sweetest.

- Look for pronouns! Remember to focus on pronouns and check for promiscuity!

For the Improving Paragraphs Section:

- **Do all the "grammar-ish" questions first** – skip any context or unity questions and save them for last!

- For the context/unity sentences **think transitions and main idea.**

- Skip over "Choice A", since this is the same as the original question, and look at the other answer choices first.

- In this section, **pronouns should be eliminated.** For example, instead of picking an answer choice with "he" in it, pick an answer choice with "Michael".

> **The grammar section is like a poker game. There are good hands and there are really good hands. Likewise, there are grammatical errors and there are really bad grammatical errors. Subject - Verb agreement and pronoun errors trump the other "Key" errors.**

The Winning ACT Strategy

▦ FIRST

1. Skip the thinking/context question until you've read the whole passage.
2. Skim the answer choices to see what's changing… tense, pronouns, commas, etc.
3. Don't be afraid of OMIT or NO CHANGE… there is no pattern on the ACT.

▦ THEN

▦ Look at the shortest answers first. Remember, shortest is sweetest.

▦ Look at answers with OMIT. Omitting a portion of a sentence makes it nice and short.

▦ Eliminate answers: being, where and which are usually wrong.

▦ AND REMEMBER...

▦ Comma and = period

▦ Semicolon= period

▦ Colon= definition or explanation, or introduction of a list

▦ it's = it is

▦ **A comma cannot separate 2 sentences by itself!**

▦ 2 commas = remove everything in between

The Grammar Keys Explained

Below are the keys to grammar, explained. Use this sheet as you're doing grammar sections until you have the keys pretty much down. Then, use the quick reference sheet found on the following page. ALWAYS have a key sheet out so that you're training yourself – brainwashing yourself – to look for certain repeating questions!

The SAT loves starting sentences with "because"

The SAT knows you've been told to never do this. Therefore, they do it all the time trying to TRICK you. If you see an answer choice that starts with "because", look at it FIRST. It's probably correct

Diction

One question per test, the SAT just throws in the wrong word (diction). These are often very subtle, and difficult to catch – so look out for the diction question!

Subject-verb agreement

IS/ARE
HAS/HAVE
WAS/WERE

These guys are usually switched on the test. Make sure plural subjects are paired with plural verbs. Think "he" for singular and "they" for plural nouns so that you can easily tell if the verb is singular or plural.

Shortest is Sweetest

Jump to short answer choices first. The shortest is often right!

Would vs. Will

Always look twice at these when underlined in a sentence; the SAT switches them.

TO vs. ING

Whenever you have a "to-verb" or an "ing-verb" underlined, switch them and see which sounds better. For example, if "to run" was underlined, think to yourself Would "for running" sound better? and vice versa.

Love "-LY" and hate without

Adverbs typically end in "-LY". If you see an -LY word underlined, it's probably right! (Except for HARDLY and SCARCELY.) Generally, there are 1 or 2 questions in which the -LY is left off, and those are wrong. If describing a verb (action), the word must end in -LY. For example: The snowmobile was driven cautiously, not cautious. **There will be 2-3 adverb questions per test!**

Check ALL underlined pronouns twice

Pronouns (I, he, she, it, etc.) are the number-one error on this test. Any pronoun you see should be checked, and then rechecked. You should be able to immediately pinpoint what the pronoun is referring to. If not – the pronoun is wrong.

Its vs. Their – always look twice when these words are underlined

Pronouns are very, very bad on this test. "Its" and "their" are commonly switched on the SAT. "Its" is for singular and "their" is for plural possession – so make sure you know the subject of the sentence! **Look out for "it" vs. "they" as well.**

It = VomIT – Be careful of any underlined "it"

It is commonly a vague and *promiscuous* pronoun. Double check all underlined "it"s.

It vs. They – always look twice when these words are underlined

Pronouns are a very bad thing. "It" and "they" are commonly switched on the SAT. "It" is for singular and "they" is for plural – so make sure you know the subject of the sentence! **Look twice at "it" and "they".**

Either, Neither, and Each are singular

This is a tricky one! "Either", "neither", "every", and "each" are all singular and take singular verbs. It will always sound wrong, so don't trust your ears! Know the KEY!! For example, *Neither the car nor the truck IS working…not ARE working.* Remember, think "he" when you see singular subjects so that you don't get confused!

"AND" is an equal sign

Any time you have an "and" in a sentence, make sure the sentence is balanced around it. For example: *The maid was hired to cook AND to clean…not to cook AND for cleaning.*

Than and As need to make equal comparisons

The SAT loves comparisons. Any time you see a THAN, AS, LIKE, UNLIKE, etc. make sure you're comparing apples to apples. Comparisons need to be *perfectly* equal on this test. For example: *Dante's poems are as good as Shakespeare.* **NO!** *Dante's poems are as good as Shakespeare's POEMS.* These are subtle but common SAT questions!!

More vs. Most

Any underlined "more" or "most" should be double checked. The "more" forms of comparison are used when you are dealing with two items. The "most" form is for more than two.
For example: *Jenni is TALLER than Amy.* (2 subjects)
Jenni is the TALLEST of the 4 girls. (more than 2 subjects)

Circle Numbers

A helpful clue for subject/verb, comparisons, and more vs. most is to circle numbers.

Semicolons

The SAT loves semicolons! A semicolon is, in essence, a period. If you see an answer choice with a semicolon, and you've got a full sentence on one side, and a full sentence on the other – pick that answer!

Scarcely, Any, Hardly – DOUBLE negatives

The exception to the "I love -LY rule": hardly, scarcely. Any time you see "hardly", "scarcely", "any", or "without" underlined, you're probably dealing with a double negative and it's probably wrong.

"W" keys – Where, Which, While

Where is usually wrong – only refers to direction
Which is a b!@#% – wrong unless a preposition (little word) comes before it
While is usually wrong

"Being" is BAD

If you have "being" in the sentence, it's WRONG! (Unless it says *"human being"*…)

I LOVE "That"

"That" is almost always correct. It may sound wordy, but don't pick an underlined "that".

Hand Holders – On the SAT, certain things come in pairs…

Both has to go with **And**
Not Only has to go with **But Also**
Neither goes with **Nor**
Either goes with **Or**
From goes with **To**

Grammar Keys:

▪ Check **SUBJECT-VERB AGREEMENT**
▪ Check **PRONOUN USAGE** - case, "promiscuous" pronouns

▪ **WE HATE:**
It = ugh!
Being = Bad
Is When = ugh!
Which <u>unless</u> a preposition comes before "which"
Where <u>unless</u> used for direction
Double negatives, e.g. no, any, hardly, scarcely BE CAREFUL!

▪ **WE LOVE:**
Active voice, not passive
Short and Sweet!
That (it's almost never wrong)
Of, For, To - the most common prepositions. Remember, prepositional phrases **never** contain the subject. Also, many idioms contain these prepositions.

▪ **WE NEED TO LOOK TWICE AT:**
There is/There are - usually wrong
Would & Will
This/These/Those - trouble ahead?
To-vs.-Ing - use your ear
While
Like - only use as a preposition, NOT a comparison
Each, Either, Neither - ALWAYS singular verb
Their vs. Its - their/plural, its/singular
Semicolon (;) - must have complete sentence on both sides
Numbers - look for comparative/superlative or noun agreement
Both - married to And, either/or, neither/nor
Comparisons (e.g. than, as) - must be parallel on both sides
Conjunctions (and, or, but, nor, for, so) - must be parallel on both sides
1 Diction (i.e. word choice) question per test
1 Adverb question per test

Remember, it's just like a Poker Game...Subject-Verb Agreement TRUMPS all!

**Another quick 'n' handy cheat sheet –
formatted to follow the book, key by key.**

A Grammar Key Checklist:

- The SAT loves starting sentences with "because"
- Always reduce a complex sentence to its simplest, basic form
- Always check subject-verb agreement first
- Think "he" for singular nouns and "they" for plural so that you can easily hear subject-verb errors.
- There is/There are, There has/There have, There was/There were
- Shortest is Sweetest
- WOULD vs. WILL Always look twice at these when underlined in a sentence
- TO-vs.-ING
- 1-2 Adverb questions per test
- Watch out for promiscuous pronouns
- Check ALL underlined pronouns twice
- It = Vomit
- IT vs. THEY – always look twice when these words are underlined
- "EITHER", "NEITHER", and "EACH" are singular
- "AND" is an equal sign
- "THAN" and "AS" need to make equal comparisons
- Shortest and Sweetest does not apply to comparisons
- More vs. Most
- Circle Numbers
- A semicolon must have a complete sentence on either side
- "SCARCELY", "ANY", "HARDLY" and "NO" create double negatives
- Diction errors occur once per exam
- Memorize the "W" keys – Where, Which, While
    - Where is usually wrong
    - Which is a b%@#!... It is wrong unless a preposition comes before it
- "BEING" is wrong on this test!
- "THAT" is usually correct on this test!
- "No Error" is 1 out of 5 – don't be afraid to pick "No error"
    - (but check your prepositions first for idioms!)

Grammar Workbook

The following pages include various worksheets for you to practice and perfect the areas of grammar most commonly tested on the SAT and ACT. Complete these worksheets after reading *English in English* to implement the tools and strategies presented in the book.

Sentence Stripping Worksheet

Write the "stripped" version of each sentence. Correct any errors in agreement.

1. Others on the team, like the captain Brian Smalley, is concerned about the lack of team spirit.

   _____

   _____

2. The waiters' professionalism – especially their knowledge of wine, their meticulousness and their pleasant attitudes – are what makes the restaurant a five-star dining experience.

   _____

   _____

3. The large number of teachers that quit after their first year contribute to an intimidating professional environment.

   _____

   _____

4. When anthropologists hypothesize about cultural similarities, they must be fully aware of the fact that these similarities have evolved over millennia.

   _____

   _____

5. One in every three smokers agree strongly with the statement: "Anyone who tries to quit smoking would succeed."

   _____

   _____

6. The fact that sharks have been responsible for so few human deaths have forced scientists to rethink the nickname "man-eater."

   _____

   _____

7. Balancing the demands of both sports and my music rehearsals often seem too much to handle.

   _____

   _____

Subject-Verb Agreement Worksheet

Label each verb in the sentences below with a 'V' and each subject with an 'S'. Correct any errors in subject-verb agreement.

1. We were astonished to discover that there was two new planets discovered.

   _____

   _____

2. Either the principal or his secretary are going to announce the school closing.

   _____

   _____

3. There is usually two or three guard dogs at the cemetery.

   _____

   _____

4. Each player on both the Little Giants and Big Reds are going to Mike's after party.

   _____

   _____

5. There has been a grocery store and a pharmacy in the plaza ever since it was established.

   _____

   _____

6. Either Thomas or John are starring as the lead in the play.

   _____

   _____

7. There is no fewer than nine people attending.

   _____

   _____

8. The counseling can continue as scheduled because neither of the spouses are sensitive to criticism.

   _____

   _____

9. There is more than two years of college remaining before she graduates.

   _____

   _____

10. Neither of the campers were frightened by the howling wolf.

   _____

   _____

11. Every teacher in both schools were concerned about the union meeting.

   _____

   _____

Tense Worksheet

Correct any tense errors in the following sentences.

1. By the time the Senate had adjourned the meeting, it voted against six huge proposals.

   _____

   _____

2. In the morning, we had a delicious brunch with the same people we hiked with the day before.

   _____

   _____

3. By the time my thesis is approved, I will write at least three revisions.

   _____

   _____

4. Being nominated for class president, Sara felt that she had to promise school reform.

   _____

   _____

5. It surprised us to learn that reptiles were closely related to birds.

   _____

   _____

6. Reading Fredrick Douglas' autobiography, I feel as if I've gained insight into the horrors of slavery.

   _____

   _____

7. When the hurricane hit Louisiana, the entire population had suffered.

   _____

   _____

8. I have never felt so free as when I am painting.

   _____

   _____

9. Centuries ago, people believed that sicknesses were caused by curses and magic.

   _____

   _____

10. Roger has been the manager of the restaurant ever since it was opened.

   _____

   _____

11. Over the last three years, stock values have decreased by over 12 percent.

_____

_____

12. Models often worry excessively about weight and will forget about actually being healthy.

_____

_____

13. We need not bother repairing the transmission now that the entire engine had been destroyed.

_____

_____

14. We will have been with this company for three years in May.

_____

_____

15. By the time we arrived at the park where the reunion would be held, the caterers cleared all the tables.

_____

_____

Pronoun Agreement Worksheet

Correct any errors in pronouns in the sentences below. Sentences may be correct as is.

1. Although the team trained for hours on end for the race, they quickly became tired.
   _____
   _____

2. Cornell has prided itself on their commitment to providing students with rigorous academia.
   _____
   _____

3. Each of the girls wanted their choreography to be used in the new dance.
   _____
   _____

4. No one who starts the diet and exercise program ever believes that they will lose weight.
   _____
   _____

5. Although you shouldn't be too stingy, one doesn't need to overspend, either.
   _____
   _____

6. Neither med student thought that they would see such trauma.
   _____
   _____

7. They usually award first place to the painting that shows the most artistic creativity.
   _____
   _____

8. The museum received so many artifacts that they had to build an additional display case.
   _____
   _____

9. Everybody is expected to contribute their $50 to the limo.
   _____

10. Teenagers aren't prepared for the responsibilities that accompany getting his or her driving license.
    _____
    _____

11. The committee had decided that they would meet the first of every month.

_____

_____

12. Each racer will have a lane to themselves.

_____

_____

Pronoun Case Worksheet

Choose the correct pronoun in each of the following sentences

1. The committee presented the honor to Michael and (he/him).

2. After the tournament, everyone agreed that no one had played harder than (her/she).

3. Jaclyn and (me/I) have known one another for 16 years.

4. There is no point in (our/us) delaying the meeting any longer.

5. I shall give free passes to (he/him) who can answer the next trivia question correctly.

6. It seems obvious that you and (me/I) will have to cooperate in order to complete the task.

7. It's going to be difficult for (he and I/him and me) to agree on a birthday present for Dad.

8. The other dancers and (her/she) needed to practice for tomorrow's recital.

9. The school board was thrilled about (he/his) agreeing to speak at graduation.

10. (We/Us) and the other fans placed bets on which team would win the game.

11. The restaurant manager offered my sister and (me/I) a complimentary bottle of champagne.

12. No other student in the class could speak as fluently as (myself/me/I).

13. The teachers were getting tired of (him/his) constantly disrupting class.

14. The riverbank always held a special attraction for Samantha and (me/I).

15. Between you and (I/me) there are no secrets.

Parallelism Worksheet

In the following sentences, correct any problems with parallelism.

1. Aerobics classes are not only beneficial, but they also entertain.

   _____

   _____

2. Filing taxes is about as much fun as when you watch paint dry.

   _____

   _____

3. My instructor was more concerned about the assignment was finished on time than about the assignment being done correctly.

   _____

   _____

4. To say she is outspoken is like saying Michael Jordan is athletic.

   _____

   _____

5. The composition of the piece was incredible, but I thought the technique was less than impressive.

   _____

   _____

6. The popularity of a song lies more in its catchiness and beat than in how meaningful the lyrics are.

   _____

   _____

7. Cinderella swept the floors, washed the windows, and she mopped the kitchen herself.

   _____

   _____

8. Astronaut training involves physical exertion, mental exercises, and practicing orientation.

   _____

   _____

9. The opponents were neither strategically prepared nor did they have any discipline.

   _____

10. The chef was concerned not only with good taste, but also wanted to have good presentation.

    _____

    _____

11. Parents often prefer to pay high school taxes than to the paying of high tuition.

_____

_____

12. Flying through that storm was like a ride on a roller coaster.

_____

_____

13. As a coach, he loved to motivate players even more than he loved winning games.

_____

_____

Comparison Worksheet

Correct any errors in the comparisons below.

1. I prefer modern music to Beethoven.

   _____

2. The anatomy of a cat arm differs only slightly from a human.

   _____

3. She has more clothes than me.

   _____

4. Many children want to be an astronaut.

   _____

   _____

5. Mr. Norselli's comments, like so many other professors, did not take into consideration the feelings of the students.

   _____

   _____

6. The executive liked Clayton's proposal better than his coworker Jon.

   _____

7. Even in today's society, minority groups are treated as an inferior.

   _____

8. Even in the 21st century, the salaries of women are lower than men.

   _____

9. Unlike most mystery novels, Agatha Christie writes stories that in some cases are never solved.

   _____

   _____

10. Some critics argue that Picasso's paintings are more thought provoking than Monet.

    _____

    _____

11. According to the votes, the majority of the tasting panel liked Sally's cake better than Martha.

    _____

    _____

12. In modern society, unlike the past, women are fully integrated into the workforce.

    _____

    _____

Idiom Worksheet

Insert the correct prepositions below to make the sentences idiomatic.

1. The program provided insight _____ what great artists think about.

2. We were very angry _____ her for failing the test.

3. The new survey had questions that seemed very different _____ those that have been on previous surveys.

4. My instructor preferred my drawing _____ my painting.

5. The officers ran _____ pursuit _____ the suspects.

6. When she moved into her new apartment, she felt completely independent _____ her parents.

7. The detectives combed the room in search _____ clues.

8. Although they were professionals, the two doctors always seemed to be arguing _____ each other.

9. It was hard not to agree _____ the manager's offer of a free dinner for two.

10. If we don't submit our paperwork immediately, we may miss _____ the opportunity to participate.

11. The extracurricular points were given to everyone who worked on the project _____ evolution.

Dangling Modification Worksheet

Choose the answer that corrects the underlined portions of the sentences below.

1. While volunteering at a shelter downtown, <u>that was when Sarah developed a profound love for the poor.</u>
    a. that was when Sarah developed a profound love for the poor.
    b. Sarah developed a profound love for the poor.
    c. then the development of Sarah's profound love for the poor took place.
    d. Sarah's profound love for the poor developed.
    e. a profound love for the poor developed in Sarah.

2. Like most tourists, <u>the city's strange traffic signs confused the Smith family.</u>
    a. the city's strange traffic signs confused the Smith family.
    b. the strange traffic signs in the city confused the Smith family.
    c. the Smith family was confused by the city's strange traffic signs.
    d. the Smith family, who found the city's strange traffic signs confusing.
    e. there were strange traffic signs in the city, which confused the Smith family.

3. Besides having sold millions of CDs, <u>inspiration was provided by Ice-T to many aspiring rap artists living in inner cities.</u>
    a. inspiration was provided by Ice-T to many aspiring rap artists living in inner cities.
    b. many aspiring rap artists living in inner cities received inspiration from Ice-T.
    c. Ice-T's inspiration was provided to many aspiring rap artists living in inner cities.
    d. and while Ice-T inspired many aspiring rap artists living in inner cities.
    e. Ice-T has inspired many aspiring rap artists living in inner cities.

4. Costing much less than the process of wood pulping, <u>a fourth of our total paper supply is now provided by recycling.</u>
    a. a fourth of our total paper supply is now provided by recycling.
    b. of our total supply of paper, a fourth is now provided by recycling.
    c. we now produce a fourth of our total paper supply through recycling.
    d. recycling now provides a fourth of our total paper supply.
    e. our total paper supply from recycling process about a fourth.

5. Lecturing to the graduating class, <u>read the works of Charles Dickens was the advice Professor Mathews gave.</u>
    a. read the works of Charles Dickens was the advice Professor Mathews gave.
    b. the works of Charles Dickens was what Professor Mathews gave.
    c. the audience was advised to read the works of Charles Dickens by Professor Mathews.
    d. Charles Dickens' works, advised by Professor Mathews, was what the audience should read.
    e. Professor Mathews advised to read the works of Charles Dickens.

6.   Once a prevalent cause of death in the United States, <u>the use of an effective vaccine has nearly expunged polio from the United States.</u>
   a.   the use of an effective vaccine has nearly expunged polio from the United States.
   b.   through the use of an effective vaccine, polio has been nearly expunged from the United States.
   c.   the near expunging of polio in the United States has been achieved through an effective vaccine.
   d.   polio has been nearly expunged from the United States through the use of an effective vaccine.
   e.   polio has nearly been expunged from the United States, being that there is an effective vaccine.

7.   To ensure that the cola will have the same carbonation from liter to liter, <u>it is the quality control specialist who checks random samples of liquid from each lot.</u>
   a.   it is the quality control specialist who checks random samples of liquid from each lot.
   b.   the quality control specialist checks random samples of liquid from each lot.
   c.   random samples of liquid are taken from each lot by the quality control specialist.
   d.   the quality control specialist checks samples of liquid, being at random, from each lot.
   e.   the quality control specialist is checking random samples of liquid from each lot.

Apostrophe Worksheet

Place apostrophes where they belong in the following sentences. Sentences may require no, one, or more than one apostrophe.

1. Im not going tomorrow.
    I'm not going tomorrow.

2. Have you received Janices term paper yet?
    Janice's

3. Mens Warehouse also carries childrens clothing.
    *Men's   children's**

4. Johns store carries only boys' clothes.
    John's

5. The families vacation home was vandalized by the Smith family's children.

6. My brother-in-law's sister works with the city's government.

7. Japan's closed-door policy affected America's and Europe's trade industries.

8. The babies at the daycare were disturbed by one baby's crying.
    baby's

9. It's not as hot as it looks.

10. Its mouth looked big enough to swallow me whole.

11. The player's equipment was left in his locker.

12. Shanella's pen ran out of ink as soon as the proctors' said to begin.

13. Sam is going on a week's vacation.

14. Today's work will be much harder than yesterday's.

Punctuation Worksheet

Insert punctuation into the following sentences. Semicolons, colons and/or dashes may be used. Some sentences require multiple punctuation marks.

1. The men on trial, Sam Cullot, Cory Mazz, and Marcus Brymm deserve awards.

    trial — Sam . . . . Brymm — deserve . . .

2. Several countries signed the treaty Italy, France, England and Spain.

    treaty:

3. Only one option was left; the other choices were already taken by other members.

4. Willy Mays, later to be inducted into the Baseball Hall of Fame, once struggled to make the Giants' team.

5. After that day, Martha never looked back; her son was born three months later.

6. The most prevalent element in the atmosphere is nitrogen about 71 percent.

    nitrogen: about

7. Mary refused to ride the Ferris wheel; her sister, however, was first in line.

8. When I was younger my father took me on all sorts of fishing trips Texas, Maryland, Boston but now we rarely go.

    trips — Texas . . . .
    Boston — but . . .

9. The office was cleaned every Friday evening; after the work week it looked disastrous.

10. First the woman read her a story; then she gave her a glass of milk.

SAT Worksheet #1

The following questions are modeled after SAT-style grammar questions. Circle the underlined portion of the sentence with the error. If you do not think there is an error, circle "No error". Remember, you do not have to correct errors, only find them.

1. Louisa May Alcott, <u>among</u> others, <u>are known</u> for <u>writing from</u> a woman's viewpoint. <u>No error.</u>

2. <u>The</u> wonderful <u>school yearbook was</u> edited by Carl and <u>she</u>. <u>No error.</u>

3. <u>There</u> <u>wasn't scarcely</u> <u>any</u> money left <u>in</u> the club's treasury. <u>No error.</u>

4. They <u>choosed</u> not <u>to take</u> <u>the train</u> into <u>Manhattan</u>. <u>No error.</u>

5. A <u>box</u> of materials <u>are</u> in <u>the cabinet</u> on <u>the right</u>. <u>No error.</u>

6. <u>Between</u> you and <u>I</u>, the future <u>looks bright</u>. <u>No error.</u>

7. <u>Jogging</u> will <u>take off</u> <u>fewer pounds</u> than <u>to eat</u> properly. <u>No error.</u>

8. <u>Although</u> <u>he has been</u> here <u>only</u> two weeks, he <u>saw</u> all the important sights. <u>No error.</u>

9. Even plants <u>which</u> <u>serve</u> <u>to decorate</u> a home <u>can be</u> dangerous. <u>No error.</u>

10. Someone <u>might</u> <u>take</u> the wrong pill if <u>they</u> did not <u>read</u> the labels. <u>No error.</u>

11. <u>To become</u> a world figure-skating champion like Kristi Yamaguchi, one <u>must be</u> so dedicated that <u>you</u> <u>will practice</u> six hours a day. <u>No error.</u>

12. Information about some pollutants is difficult <u>in gathering</u> <u>because</u> the effects <u>of those</u> pollutants on human health are often not <u>immediately</u> apparent. <u>No error.</u>

13. <u>Neither</u> the <u>issue of</u> pollution nor the resulting problem of acid rain <u>were</u> even <u>mentioned in</u> the candidate's campaign speech. <u>No error.</u>

14. Photographs of genetic molecules have revealed how <u>close</u> the images of DNA resemble the theoretical model that scientists <u>have used</u> <u>for</u> <u>so long</u>. <u>No error.</u>

15. Charles Dickens' novel *Great Expectations* <u>focuses on</u> the character Pip, who as a young adult has <u>scarcely no</u> <u>understanding</u> of his <u>own</u> origins. <u>No error.</u>

16. Of the two speakers, Maria was <u>the least</u> apprehensive <u>about appearing</u> before an audience, <u>for she had</u> <u>done so</u> several times before. <u>No error.</u>

17. There has always been <u>a great deal</u> of friction between <u>Joan and I</u> <u>because we</u> have opposing political views <u>about which</u> we are very vocal. <u>No error.</u>

18. The flowers that Jan and Jonathan <u>ordered</u> to be sent <u>to their mother</u> were <u>less</u> fresh and much more expensive than <u>Carr's Flower Shop</u>. <u>No error.</u>

19. To ensure <u>the safety</u> of the employees, the managers of the company schedule monthly fire drills <u>in which</u> the entire staff <u>had to participate</u>. <u>No error.</u>

20. <u>In her summary</u>, the speaker <u>stressed that</u> the group's <u>primary</u> goal is equity, both in social relations <u>as well as</u> business opportunities. <u>No error.</u>

21. <u>It is</u> true that the processes of problem solving in some advanced computer programs <u>are</u> virtually the same <u>as the mind</u>. <u>No error.</u>

22. Any exhibition of Polish artwork <u>would show</u> clearly that the ancient traditions of Poland <u>are</u> <u>preserved</u> in <u>their</u> art. <u>No error.</u>

23. The adviser's suggestion <u>included</u> a plan <u>where</u> each of the countries was <u>to</u> <u>improve its</u> economy by cooperating with the others. <u>No error.</u>

SAT Worksheet #2

Below is an SAT-style Grammar test. Choose the answer that best expresses the meaning of the original sentence. "Choice a" is always the original sentence.

1. Agatha Christie's new mystery does not offer timeless literary themes, <u>but one that does offer considerable</u> entertainment.
    a. but one that does offer
    b. but it does offer
    c. but that does offer
    d. however offering
    e. however that does offer

2. Many fishermen <u>work unceasing for catching</u> the number of fish the market demands.
    a. work unceasing for catching
    b. work unceasing to catch
    c. work to catch unceasingly
    d. work unceasingly for catching
    e. work unceasingly to catch

3. Miranda was anxious before her recital, <u>having shown confidence once the performance got</u> under way.
    a. having shown confidence once the performance got
    b. but she showed confidence once the performance got
    c. but showing confidence once the performance got
    d. once she showed confidence when the performance got
    e. however, she showed confidence when the performance had been

4. Strolling beneath the palm trees on the beach, <u>right above them a parrot swooped down.</u>
    a. right above them a parrot swooped down.
    b. there was a parrot swooping right above them.
    c. a parrot swooped down right above them.
    d. they saw a parrot swoop down above them.
    e. they saw right above them a parrot swoop down.

5. The boy's obnoxious behavior <u>had been frustrating to some and he was</u> better behaved after several unpleasant encounters.
    a. had been frustrating to some and he
    b. had been frustrating to some; but he had been
    c. had been frustrating to some; however, he became
    d. frustrated some, while he was
    e. frustrated some, however he became

6. Juggling multiple extracurricular activities is quite common among high school students, the majority <u>of them play</u> sports and a musical instrument.
    a. of them play
    b. of them are playing
    c. which play
    d. of whom play
    e. play

7. Fires blazed across California, incinerating <u>forests and homes were burned along the border.</u>
    a. forests and homes were burned along the border.
    b. forests and with the homes being burned along the border.
    c. forests, and the burning of homes was witnessed along the border.
    d. forests and burning the homes along the border.
    e. forests; burning along the border the homes.

8. Suffering from a twisted ankle, <u>Michelle's search for a taxi was frantic.</u>
    a. Michelle's search for a taxi was frantic.
    b. Michelle's frantic search was for a taxi.
    c. a taxi was what Michelle frantically searched for.
    d. a taxi for which Michelle frantically searched.
    e. Michelle searched frantically for a taxi.

9. Accustomed to the hustle and bustle of city life, <u>it was only when I moved to rural Texas that I understood what quiet really was.</u>
    a. it was only when I moved to rural Texas that I understood what quiet really was.
    b. when I moved to rural Texas I understood what quiet really was.
    c. moving to rural Texas taught me what quiet really was.
    d. I did not know what quiet really was until I moved to rural Texas.
    e. quiet was unknown to me until I moved to rural Texas.

10. Martin Luther King, Jr.'s "Letter from Birmingham Jail" is often studied in composition <u>classes and it is</u> a model of persuasive argument.
    a. classes and it is
    b. classes, when it is
    c. classes as
    d. classes; moreover as
    e. classes whereas it is

11. Because bicycling has become <u>so popular is the reason that some cities have established bicycle lanes.</u>
   a. popular is the reason that some cities have established bicycle lanes.
   b. popular, some cities have established bicycle lanes.
   c. popular, there has been bicycle lanes.
   d. popular is the reason that bicycle lanes have been established in some cities.
   e. popular, they have established bicycle lanes in some cities.

12. <u>A native New Yorker, Gloria Naylor's first novel won</u> an American Book Award in 1983.
   a. A native New Yorker, Gloria Naylor's first novel won
   b. A native New Yorker, the first novel by Gloria Naylor won
   c. The first novel by Gloria Naylor, a native New Yorker, won
   d. Gloria Naylor, a native New Yorker, wrote her first novel and she won
   e. A native New Yorker, Gloria Naylor as well as her first novel won

13. Jack was disappointed because his score on the test <u>was not as outstanding as Rob.</u>
   a. was not as outstanding as Rob.
   b. did not stand out as much as Rob.
   c. was not as outstanding as Rob's.
   d. did not surpass Rob.
   e. was not as outstanding than Rob's.

14. Holding up the bill in Congress, <u>many problems were caused by the lobbyist.</u>
   a. many problems were caused by the lobbyist.
   b. the lobbyist caused many problems.
   c. problems resulted, there were many of them, because of the lobbyist.
   d. causing many problems was the lobbyist.
   e. the lobbyist was the cause of many problems.

15. Running to home plate, <u>the game was ended by Strawberry.</u>
   a. the game was ended by Strawberry.
   b. the end of the game was caused by Strawberry.
   c. Strawberry ended the game.
   d. Strawberry was ending the game.
   e. Strawberry had ended the game.

SAT Practice Worksheet #3

The following questions are modeled after SAT-style grammar questions. Circle the underlined portion of the sentence with the error. If you do not think there is an error, circle "No error". Remember, you do not have to correct errors, only find them.

1. If Shakespeare were alive today, <u>he would</u>, <u>without hardly</u> a doubt, not want his name <u>associated with</u> last night's <u>presentation of</u> "Hamlet." <u>No error.</u>

2. <u>Dylan's turned thirty</u>, and the Beatles' breaking up, <u>signified</u> the end of a distinctive period <u>in</u> rock music. <u>No error.</u>

3. Rather than discussing the issues <u>on which</u> this campaign <u>should be decided</u>, Mr. Richards <u>resorts to</u> insult, exaggeration, <u>and he lies</u>. <u>No error.</u>

4. Sarah and her roommate <u>planned to</u> be <u>a candidate</u> for class president, <u>even though</u> their course work <u>was very demanding</u>. <u>No error.</u>

5. A housing crisis <u>developed when</u> farm workers <u>which</u> were seeking economic security came to the city <u>looking</u> for jobs. <u>No error.</u>

6. The discussion between Professor Barron <u>and I</u> centered on <u>what we thought</u> Hitler would have done <u>had he known</u> <u>how weak</u> England was in 1940. <u>No error.</u>

7. O'Neil <u>experimented with</u> <u>each of</u> his plays, <u>skillfully</u> choosing difficult subjects and <u>he would employ</u> unusual dramatic techniques. <u>No error.</u>

8. Every one of the city's newspapers <u>have</u> urged its readers <u>to vote</u> <u>in</u> the special election <u>to be held</u> on Tuesday. <u>No error.</u>

9. <u>Although</u> Ellen is a better tennis player than <u>him</u>, Henry insists on competing <u>with her</u> and <u>usually loses</u>. <u>No error.</u>

10. <u>Once regarded</u> as "Africa's Guiding Light," Kwame Nkrumah <u>helped</u> the West African colonies win independence <u>and serving</u> as the first prime minister <u>of Ghana</u>. <u>No error.</u>

11. Nature <u>has</u> served Russia <u>harshly</u> in at least one respect: seven-eighths of <u>their vast country</u> lies <u>in</u> the cold latitudes. <u>No error.</u>

12. Even <u>to work</u> diligently in the garden has not prevented the hardiest weeds from springing up again and again. <u>No error.</u>

13. Freud <u>suggests that</u> there is no such thing <u>as</u> a slip of the tongue, for <u>they are</u> actually what the subconscious mind <u>intends us</u> to say. <u>No error.</u>

14. The early natural scientist <u>did not</u> <u>doubt that</u> there were unicorns, <u>even though</u> he <u>never sees</u> one. <u>No error.</u>

15. Jane Austen, <u>unlike</u> many of her contemporaries, <u>cannot be called</u> a sentimentalist; <u>in fact</u> she mocked <u>it</u> in her novels. <u>No error.</u>

ACT Worksheet

The following worksheet provides specific ACT-style grammar questions.

Family Rivalry

I

There is an ongoing dispute <u>fighting around</u>

1

my family, a group that was once close-knit and peaceful. The cause of the dispute is <u>my</u>
<u>uncle's being drafted</u> into the minor baseball

2

leagues and the root of the problem is my father's –
<u>his twin brother's – jealousy.</u>

3

<u>Because they are twins, and share the same birthday,</u>
<u>my father and uncle have been in constant</u>
<u>competition.</u>

4

II

During college, the competition <u>escalated.</u>

5

Both of them <u>were in</u> the college baseball

6

team and both of them were <u>as equally good.</u>

7

During games the coach would let my father play the first half of the <u>game, and my</u> uncle

8

play the second half. 9

1. A) NO CHANGE
   B) surrounding
   C) undertaking
   D) within

2. A) NO CHANGE
   B) that my uncle was drafted
   C) my uncle's drafting
   D) my uncles draft into

3. A) NO CHANGE
   B) his twin brothers' –
   C) his twin brothers',
   D) his twin brother's,

4. A) NO CHANGE
   B) Because they are twins, my father and uncle
      have been in constant competition.
   C) Being in constant competition because they
      are twins, which means they have the same
      birthday.
   D) Because they are twins – born on the same day
      – they have been constantly competing.

5. A) NO CHANGE
   B) skyrocketed
   C) exploded
   D) increased

6. A) NO CHANGE
   B) were on
   C) were, on
   D) were, in

7. A) NO CHANGE
   B) as equals, good.
   C) equally as good.
   D) equally good.

8. A) NO CHANGE
   B) game; my
   C) game. My
   D) game and my

9. At this point the author is considering adding the
   following sentence:
   A baseball game normally consists of nine innings.
   Should the author make this addition?

   A) No; the additional details are not revelant to the
      main point of the passage
   B) No; the addition should be made earlier to clarify
      the rules of baseball
   C) Yes; the addition helps the reader understand why
      the uncle and father were in competition
   D) Yes; the detail provided is an interesting fact.

III

However, one day my father was ill – he had a virus,
                                            10
and could not play. This happened to be the day that
a scout from minor leagues was recruiting potential
players.   My uncle played flawless the entire
                              11
game and was immediately signed to play: with the
                                          12
Red Wings. Unfortunately for my father, the scout
did not get to see him play, and therefore, did not
                              13

consider him, for the minor leagues.
           14

IV

And so, the family controversy began. My father
      15
refused to invite my uncle to family outings like

picnics and barbeques; birthdays and holidays. My
                  16

uncle mails my father, through the postal system,
                          17

videos of all of his games. He likes to taunt my father

with his success, and my father likes to taunt him
            18

back to watch only football and hockey.
       19

V

(1) When my grandfather was sick both of them were
at the hospital together. (2) Despite the baseball
rivalry, I know deep down that my father and uncle
support each other. (3) Since, I'm
                    20
still not allowed to watch any baseball in the house.

10. A) NO CHANGE
    B) ill – he had a virus –
    C) ill,
    D) ill, being that he had a virus,

11. A) NO CHANGE
    B) played ,flawlessly,
    C) flawlessly, played
    D) played flawlessly

12. A) NO CHANGE
    B) play with
    C) play, with
    D) play, with,

13. A) NO CHANGE
    B) and, therefore
    C) and therefore;
    D) and therefore

14. A) NO CHANGE
    B) him, for the minor, changes.
    C) him for the minor changes
    D) him for: the minor changes

15. A) NO CHANGE
    B) Meanwhile,
    C) Nonetheless,
    D) OMIT the underlined portion

16. A) NO CHANGE
    B) like: picnics, barbeques, birthdays and holidays.
    C) like picnics and barbeques; birthdays and holidays
    D) like picnics, barbeques, birthdays, and holidays.

17. A) NO CHANGE
    B) using his local post office,
    C) putting in the mailbox,
    D) OMIT the underlined portion

18. A) NO CHANGE
    B) success and,
    C) success and
    D) success, and,

19. A) NO CHANGE
    B) because he watches
    C) by watching
    D) when he watches

20. A) NO CHANGE
    B) Therefore,
    C) However,
    D) OMIT the underlined portion

21. To ensure logic and cohesion of writing, where
    should sentence 1 of paragraph V be placed?

    A) where it is now
    B) after sentence 2
    C) after sentence 3
    D) the sentence does not belong in paragraph V

Answer Key

Sentence Stripping Answer Key

1. Others **are** concerned about the lack.
2. The waiter's professionalism **is** what makes the restaurant a five-star dining experience.
3. The large number **contributes**.
4. They must be fully aware that these similarities have evolved. **No error.**
5. One **agrees** strongly.
6. The fact that sharks have been responsible **has** forced scientists.
7. Balancing the demands often **seems** too much.

Subject-Verb Agreement

1. S – two new planets
V – was
V – corrected: were

2. S – Either
V – are
V – corrected: is

3. S – guard dogs
V – is
V – corrected: are

4. S – Each
V – are
V – corrected: is

5. S – Grocery store and Pharmacy
V – has
V – corrected: have

6. S – Either
V – are
V – corrected: is

7. S – People
V – is
V – corrected: are

8. S – Neither
V – are
V – corrected: is

9. S – Years
V – is
V – corrected: are

10: S – neither
V – were
V – corrected: was

11. S – Every teacher
V – were
V – corrected: was

Tense Worksheet

1. By the time the Senate had adjourned the meeting, it **had voted**...
2. ...we had a delicious brunch with the same people we **had hiked with**...
3. By the time my thesis is approved, I **will have written**...
4. No error.
5. It surprised us to learn that reptiles **are** closely related to birds.
6. No error.
7. When the hurricane hit Louisiana, the entire population **suffered**.
8. I **never feel** so free as when I am painting.
   I have never felt so free as when **I was painting**.
9. No error.
10. Roger has been the manager of the restaurant ever since **it opened**.
11. No error.
12. Models often worry...**and forget** about actually being healthy.
13. ...now that the engine **has been** destroyed.
14. No error.
15. By the time we arrived at the park where the reunion **was** held, the caterers **had cleared** all the tables.

Pronoun Agreement

1. *Although the team trained for hours on end for the race,* **it** *quickly became tired.*
2. *Cornell has prided itself on* **its** *commitment to providing students...*
3. *Each of the girls wanted* **her** *choreography to be used in the new dance.*
4. *No one who starts the diet ever believes that* **he or she** *will lose weight.*
5. *Although* **one** *shouldn't be too stingy, one shouldn't overspend, either.*
   Although you shouldn't be too stingy, **you** *shouldn't overspend, either.*
6. *Neither med student thought that* **he or she** *would see such trauma.*
7. **They** *usually award first place to the painting that shows the most artistic creativity.*
   "They" is vague here and needs to be replaced with a noun: the judges, the board, the committee, etc.
8. *The museum received so many artifacts that* **it** *had to build an additional display case.*
9. *Everybody is expected to contribute* **his or her** *$50 to the limo.*
10. *Teenagers aren't prepared for the responsibilities that accompany getting* **their** *license.*
11. *The committee decided that* **it** *would meet the first of every month.*
12. *Each racer will have a lane to* **himself or herself**.

Pronoun Case Worksheet

1. him	6. I	11. me
2. she	7. him and me	12. I
3. I	8. she	13. his
4. our	9. his	14. me
5. him	10. We	15. me

Parallelism

1. *Aerobics classes are not only* **beneficial**, *but they are* **entertaining**.
2. **Filing** *taxes is about as much fun as* **watching** *paint dry.*
3. *My instructor was more concerned about* **the assignment being finished** *on time than about* **the assignment being done** *correctly.*
4. **Saying** *she is outspoken is like* **saying** *Michael Jordan is athletic.*
5. *No error*
6. *The popularity of a song lies more in its* **catchiness** *than in the* **meaningfulness** *of its lyrics.*
7. *Cinderella* **swept** *the floor,* **washed** *the windows, and* **mopped** *the kitchen.*
8. *Astronaut training involves* **physical exertion, mental exercises, and orientation practice**.
9. *The opponents were neither strategically* **prepared** *nor* **disciplined**.
10. *The chef was concerned with not only* **good taste** *but also* **good presentation**.
11. *Parents often prefer* **paying** *high school* **taxes** *than* **paying** *high tuition.*
    Parents often prefer **to pay** *high taxes than* **to pay** *high tuition.*
12. **Flying** *through that storm was like* **riding** *a roller coaster.*
13. *As a coach, he loved* **to motivate** *players even more than he loved* **to win** *games.*
    As a coach, he loved **motivating** *players even more than he loved* **winning** *games.*

Comparison Worksheet
1. *I prefer modern music to* **Beethoven's music**.
2. *The anatomy of a cat arm differs only slightly from a* **human's arm**.
3. *She has more clothes than* **I have clothes**.
4. *Many children want to be* **astronauts**.
5. *Mr. Norselli's comments, like so many other* **professors' comments**...
6. *The executive liked Clayton's proposal better than his* **coworker Jon's proposal**.
7. *Even in today's society, minority groups are treated as* **inferiors**.
8. *Even in the 21st century, the salaries of women are lower than the* **salaries of men**.
9. *Unlike most mystery* **writers**, *Agatha Christie writes stories that in some cases are never solved.*
10. *Some critics argue that Picasso's paintings are more thought provoking than* **Monet's paintings**.
11. *According to the votes, the majority of the tasting panel liked Sally's cake better than* **Martha's cake**.
12. *In modern society, unlike* **in past societies**, *women are fully integrated into the workforce.*

Idiom Worksheet
1. into
2. at
3. from
4. to
5. in, of
6. from
7. of
8. with
9. to
10. out on
11. on

Dangling Modification Worksheet
1. b
2. c
3. e
4. d
5. e
6. d
7. b

Apostrophe Worksheet
1. *I'm not going tomorrow.*
2. *Have you received Janice's term paper yet?*
3. *Men's Warehouse also carries children's clothing.*
4. *John's store carries only boys' clothes.*
5. *The families' vacation home was vandalized by the Smith family's children.*
6. *My brother-in-law's sister works with the city's government.*
7. *Japan's closed-door policy affected America's and Europe's trade industries.*
8. *The babies at the daycare were disturbed by one baby's crying.*
9. *It's not as hot as it looks.*
10. *Its mouth looked big enough to swallow me whole.*
11. *The player's equipment was left in his locker.*
12. *Shanella's pen ran out of ink as soon as the proctors said to begin.*
13. *Sam is going on a week's vacation.*
14. *Today's work will be much harder than yesterday's.*

Punctuation Worksheet

1. *The men on trial – Sam Cullot, Cory Mazz, and Marcus Brymm – deserve awards.*
2. *Several countries signed the treaty: Italy, France, England, and Spain.*
3. *Only one option was left; the other choices were already taken by other members.*
4. *Willy Mays – later to be inducted into the Baseball Hall of Fame – once struggled to make the Giants' team.*
5. *After that day Martha never looked back; her son was born 3 months later.*
6. *The most prevalent element in the atmosphere is nitrogen: about 71 percent.*
7. *Mary refused to ride the Ferris wheel; her sister, however, was first in line.*
8. *When I was younger my father took me on all sorts of fishing trips – Texas, Maryland, Boston – but now we rarely go.*
9. *The office was cleaned every Friday evening: after the work week it looked disastrous.*
10. *First the woman read her a story; then she gave her a glass of milk.*

SAT Worksheet #1

1. are known
2. her
3. wasn't scarcely
4. choosed
5. are
6. I
7. eating
8. saw
9. which
10. they
11. you
12. in gathering
13. were
14. close
15. scarcely no
16. least
17. Joan and I
18. Carr's Flower shop
19. had to participate
20. as well as
21. are
22. their
23. where

SAT Worksheet #2

1. b
2. e
3. b
4. d
5. c
6. d
7. d
8. e
9. d
10. c
11. b
12. c
13. c
14. b
15. c

SAT Worksheet #3

1. without hardly
2. Dylan's turned thirty
3. and he lies
4. a candidate
5. which
6. and I
7. he would employ
8. have
9. him
10. and serving
11. their vast country
12. to work
13. they are
14. never sees
15. it

ACT Worksheet

1. D
2. B
3. A
4. B
5. A
6. B
7. D
8. D
9. A
10. C
11. D
12. B
13. D
14. C
15. A
16. D
17. D
18. A
19. C
20. C
21. B

SAT Worksheet #1 - Answer Explanations

1. KEY – IS vs. ARE
Any time you see an underlined "is" or "are" on the SAT, double check for subject-verb agreement. In this sentence, the subject is Louisa May Alcott: singular! Therefore, you need the singular verb "is". Of course, the SAT sets a trap by putting "others" directly before "are", hoping you'll miss the mistake.

2. KEY – PRONOUNS
Pronouns are the number-one error on the SAT. Any underlined pronoun (I, he, she, it, etc.) should be triple checked! In this sentence, "she" should be replaced with "her." *The wonderful school yearbook was edited by her...*

3. KEY – DOUBLE NEGATIVES
Train yourself to spot "hardly" and "scarcely" in a sentence. When one of these words is underlined, it is usually creating a double negative and is therefore wrong.

4. "Choosed" is incorrect in this sentence, and you should immediately hear that the error. Remember, **use your ear!** If something sounds wrong, it most likely is wrong.

5. KEY – IS vs. ARE
Any time you see an underlined "is" or "are" on the SAT, double check for subject-verb agreement. In this sentence, the subject is a box: singular! Therefore, you need the singular verb "is".

6. KEY – PRONOUNS
Pronouns are the number one error on the SAT. Any underlined pronoun (I, he, she, it, etc.) should be triple checked! You MUST memorize that "between" takes "me". Again, "between" takes "me". This is a VERY common SAT question.

7. KEY – THAN
"Than" on the SAT is an equal sign. Comparisons must be perfectly equal and parallel for them to be correct. In this sentence, "jogging" is on one side. To keep the sentence balanced, "eating" should be found on the other side of the "than," not "to eat".

8. KEY – TENSE STAYS THE SAME
Ideally, tense should remain the same in any piece of writing. Make sure you keep tense as consistent as possible. In this sentence, "saw" should be changed to "has seen" to parallel "has been" found earlier in the sentence.

9. KEY – WHICH is a BI#@$
Nine times out of ten, if "which" is underlined in a sentence and is NOT preceded by a preposition, "which" is incorrect.

10. KEY – PRONOUNS

Pronouns are the number-one error on the SAT. Any underlined pronoun (I, he, she, it, etc.) should be triple checked! This sentence begins with "someone" and then switches to "they." WRONG! If you start with "someone" you end with "someone"! Watch out for pronoun promiscuity.

11. KEY – PRONOUNS

Pronouns are the number one error on the SAT. Any underlined pronoun (I, he, she, it, etc.) should be triple checked! This sentence begins with "one" and then switches to "you." WRONG! If you start with "one" you end with "one"! Watch out for pronoun promiscuity. The identical error is found in question 10.

12. KEY – TO vs. ING

Any time you have an underlined gerund or infinitive (to-verb or -ing verb), flip-flop the forms and see which sounds better. In this sentence, "to gather" sounds much better than "in gathering." Therefore, "in gathering" is incorrect.

13. KEY – NEITHER, EITHER and EACH are SINGULAR

Memorize this key! "Neither", "either", and "each" ALWAYS take the singular verb. Therefore, "were" in this sentence should be changed to "was".

14. KEY – LOVE the – LY

Words ending in –ly are classified as adverbs, and if you find one on the SAT – it's not wrong! With the exception of "hardly" and "scarcely" (double negatives), adverbs are a beautiful thing! However, once or twice the SAT will leave off that beautiful –ly ending. In this sentence, "close" should really be "closely".

15. KEY – DOUBLE NEGATIVES

Train yourself to spot "hardly" and "scarcely" in a sentence. When one of these words is underlined, it is usually creating a double negative and is therefore wrong.

16. KEY – MORE vs. MOST

Pay attention to numbers in a sentence. Whenever you're comparing two things, you always want to use the MORE form (-er). If you're comparing three or more things, you need the MOST form (-est). Therefore, of *the two speakers, Maria was the* **less** *apprehensive.*

17. KEY – PRONOUNS

Memorize that when you see "between", you should also see "me".

18. KEY – COMPARISONS

Any time you see "than", "as", "like", etc. – note the comparison! Comparisons must be completely parallel. In this sentence, you're comparing flowers to a flower shop. "Carr's Flower Shop" should be changed to *"the flowers* at Carr's Flower Shop."

19. KEY – TENSE
Tense is a growing error on the SAT. Tense should remain consistent in a sentence. In this sentence, the managers *schedule* drills that the staff *has* to participate in.

20. KEY – BOTH is married to AND
Whenever you have "both" in a sentence, it *must* be followed by "and". Likewise, "not only" must be followed by "but also", "neither"/ "nor", "either" / "or".

21. KEY – COMPARISONS
Any time you see "than", "as", "like", etc. – note the comparison! Comparisons must be completely parallel. In this sentence, you're comparing *processes in computers* AS *processes in the mind.*

22. KEY – PRONOUNS
Remember to check, recheck, and then check again any underlined pronoun. In this case, you have "their". Ask yourself, "who are they?" The answer is people in Poland, but you don't have "people" in your sentence. "Their" is therefore promiscuous, and wrong!

23. KEY – WHERE is WRONG
"Where" should be used exclusively for location and direction. "Where" is almost always used incorrectly on the SAT – keep that in mind! Unless you're referring to an actual place, don't use "where".

SAT Worksheet #2 - Answer Explanations

1. KEY – BUT is an EQUAL SIGN
Just like "and", "but" requires parallel sentence structures. *The new mystery does not offer...BUT...it does offer....* Notice how choice b creates parallelism.

2. KEY – LOVE the –LY
If you have choices with adverbs (–ly) and choices without – go with the adverb! The SAT *loves* adverbs. This limits you to choices c, d and e. You should rely on KEY: TO vs. ING to correctly choose choice e.

3. KEY – BUT is an EQUAL SIGN
Just like "and", "but" requires parallel sentence structures. *Miranda was anxious...BUT...she showed...* Again note the parallelism that the correct answer, choice b, creates.

4. KEY – MODIFICATION
Modification is the number-one error in this section, and it revolves around commas! Always note commas in this type of question on the SAT! The portion before the comma is NOT A COMPLETE SENTENCE. Therefore, it must be stuck on to the real sentence with a comma. However, for it to correctly stick, the subject of the non-sentence portion must directly follow the comma. Therefore, *Strolling beneath the palm trees...* Ask yourself who is strolling. The people! "The people" of "They" must be found directly after the comma. This leaves only choices d and e. Choice d is shorter and more direct, and therefore correct.

5. KEY – LOVE the SEMICOLON
The SAT loves using semicolons in this section. A SEMICOLON SEPARATES TWO COMPLETE SENTENCES! If you have answer choices with semicolons, look at those first. And if the semicolon separates two complete sentences, voila – you have your answer!

6. KEY – MODIFICATION/COMMA SPLICING
Comma Splicing is the grammatical error of putting two sentences together with a comma. A COMMA ALONE CAN NEVER SEPARATE TWO COMPLETE SENTENCES. Therefore, choices a, b, and e are incorrect. Choice c is out because "which" is never used for people, leaving only the correct answer, choice d.

7. KEY – AND is an EQUAL SIGN
"And" is an equal sign on the SAT, and sentences should be balanced on either side of the "and". In this case, ...*incinerating forests AND burning homes...* Notice how choice d creates parallelism.

8. KEY – MODIFICATION
Modification is the number-one error in this section, and it revolves around commas! Always note commas in this type of question on the SAT! The portion before the comma is NOT A COMPLETE SENTENCE. Therefore, it must be stuck on to the real sentence with a comma. However, for it to correctly stick, the subject of the non-sentence portion must directly follow the comma. Michelle is suffering from a twisted ankle, so Michelle must be found directly after the comma. Choice e.

9. KEY – MODIFICATION

Modification is the number-one error in this section, and it revolves around commas! Always note commas in this type of question on the SAT! The portion before the comma is NOT A COMPLETE SENTENCE. Therefore, it must be stuck on to the real sentence with a comma. However, for it to correctly stick, the subject of the non-sentence portion must directly follow the comma. The subject was accustomed to city life, so the subject (I) must be found directly after the comma.

10. KEY – SHORTEST is often SWEETEST

Look at our shorter answers first. Oftentimes the shortest answers are correct, as is the case with this question.

11. KEY – MODIFICATION

Modification is the number-one error in this section, and it revolves around commas! Always note commas in this type of question on the SAT! The portion before the comma is NOT A COMPLETE SENTENCE. Therefore, it must be stuck on to the real sentence with a comma. Therefore, it must be stuck on to the real sentence with a comma.

12. KEY – SHORTEST is often SWEETEST

Make sure to note sentences with multiple commas. Anything sandwiched between two commas should be crossed out. When this is done to choice c, the sentence becomes concise. Shortest is sweetest!

13. KEY – COMPARISONS

Comparisons must be equal, parallel. You must choose the answer that implies Jack's score is being compared to Rob's score. Therefore, choice c is correct.

14. KEY – MODIFICATION

Modification is the number-one error in this section, and it revolves around commas! Always note commas in this type of question on the SAT! The portion before the comma is NOT A COMPLETE SENTENCE. Therefore, it must be stuck on to the real sentence with a comma. However, for it to correctly stick, the subject of the non-sentence portion must directly follow the comma. The lobbyist was holding up the bill in congress, so the lobbyist must be found directly after the comma.

15. KEY – MODIFICATION

Modification is the number-one error in this section, and it revolves around commas! Always note commas in this type of question on the SAT! The portion before the comma is NOT A COMPLETE SENTENCE. Therefore, it must be stuck on to the real sentence with a comma. However, for it to correctly stick, the subject of the non-sentence portion must directly follow the comma. Strawberry was running to home plate, and so Strawberry must be found directly after the comma.

SAT Worksheet #3 - Answer Explanations

1. KEY – DOUBLE NEGATIVES
Train yourself to spot "hardly" and "scarcely" in a sentence. When one of these words is under-lined, it is usually creating a double negative and is therefore wrong.

2. KEY – AND is an EQUAL SIGN
"And" is an equal sign, meaning that sentences should be constructed in parallel around the "and". In this sentence, you have TURNED on one side and BREAKING on the other. For parallelism, the sentence should read *Dylan's turning 30 and the Beatles' breaking up...*

3. KEY – AND is an EQUAL SIGN
"And" is an equal sign, meaning that sentences should be constructed in parallel around the "and". In this sentence, you have a list: *insult, exaggeration,* AND *he lies.* In order for the list to be parallel and balanced, "he lies" should be changed to "lies".

4. KEY – CIRCLE NUMBERS
Always take note of numbers in a sentence. In this case, the number is implied – you're dealing with TWO girls. If your subject is plural, everything else must agree with this. Therefore, *Sarah and her roommate planned to be CANDIDATES...*

5. KEY – WHICH is a Bi@#$
Nine times out of ten, if "which" is underlined in a sentence and is NOT preceded by a preposition, "which" is incorrect. In this sentence, not only is "which" not preceded by a preposition, but it also refers to farmers. "Which" can never be used in reference to people. "Who" is the appropriate pronoun in this case.

6. KEY – PRONOUNS
Memorize that when you see "between", you should also see "me".

7. KEY – AND is an EQUAL SIGN
"And" is an equal sign, meaning that sentences should be constructed in parallel around the "and". In this sentence, on one side of the "and" is *choosing.* To balance the sentence, "he would employ" should be changed to *employing.* Choosing...AND...Employing: balanced!

8. KEY – HAVE vs. HAS
Any time you see an underlined "has" or "have" on the SAT, double check for subject-verb agree-ment. In this sentence, the subject is *every one*: singular! Therefore, you need the singular verb "has".

9. KEY – PROUNOUNS
Pronouns are the number-one error on the SAT. Any underlined pronoun (I, he, she, it, etc.) should be triple checked! In this sentence, the pronoun "him" should be replaced with "he". *Sarah is a better tennis player than he is a tennis player.* It is easier to catch the mistake if you finish off the comparison.

10. KEY – AND is an EQUAL SIGN

"And" is an equal sign, meaning that sentences should be constructed in parallel around the "and." On one side of the sentence you have "helped." Although "helped" is underlined, it cannot be changed to any other verb tense. Therefore, to balance around the "and", "serving" should be changed to "served".

11. KEY – PRONOUNS

Remember to check, recheck, and then check again any underlined pronoun. In this case, you have "their". Ask yourself, "who are they?" The answer is people in Russia, but you don't have "people" in your sentence. "Their" is therefore promiscuous, and wrong!

12. KEY – TO vs. ING

Any time you have an underlined gerund or infinitive (to-verb or -ing verb), flip-flop the forms and see which sounds better. In this sentence, changing "to work" to "working" sounds much better. Therefore, "to work" is incorrect.

13. KEY – PRONOUNS

Pronouns are the number-one error on the SAT. Any underlined pronoun (I, he, she, it, etc.) should be triple checked! "They" refers to SLIPS of the tongue, but in this sentence, the subject is A SLIP of the tongue. "They" should be replaced by "it".

14. KEY – TENSE

Tense is a difficult error to catch. You need to have the ear for it. Often the SAT tries to give you clues as to what tense a sentence should be by putting dates in the sentence. ALWAYS pay attention to dates. This sentence, however, does not give you any help at all. "Never sees" should be changed to "had never seen".

15. KEY – PRONOUNS

Pronouns are the number-one error on the SAT. Any underlined pronoun (I, he, she, it, etc.) should be triple checked! "It" in this sentence is incorrect because it refers to sentimentalism. But, sentimentalism is not found in the sentence anywhere – you can't have a pronoun referring to an absent noun! This is pronoun promiscuity, and this is very wrong.